UNLIMITED
RICHES

Also by Mark Victor Hansen

BOOKS

AUDIOS

UNLIMITED RICHES

CREATING YOUR SELF-REPLENISHING PROSPERITY

MARK VICTOR HANSEN

Published 2021 by Gildan Media LLC
aka G&D Media
www.GandDmedia.com

Front cover design by David Rheinhardt of Pyrographx

Interior design by Meghan Day Healey of Story Horse, LLC

Library of Congress Cataloging-in-Publication Data is available upon request

ISBN: 978-1-7225-0360-4

10   9   8   7   6   5   4   3   2   1

Contents

Preface

Welcome to inventing a life of unlimited riches and creating self-replenishing prosperity. I like to start with simple, understandable, and instantly usable definitions to share with you the directional compass and the results you can expect from studying and taking ownership of the ideas in this book.

Unlimited means not limited or restricted in quantity, quality, extent, or numbers and potentially positively exploring an infinite number of solutions.

Riches means large amounts of money, possessions, goods, valuables, resources, assets, or supplies available to use or choose.

Creating means to originate, to bring into existence, thus cause to exist, manufacture, or produce with your mind, imagination, skills, or talents.

Self means your identity deep down. Here we are working on creating your ideal self.

Replenishing means to freshly supply what is lacking and restore completely and sustainably.

Prosperity means a state of being successful, especially with money. It is being able to attain wealth, live a luxurious lifestyle, and thrive as the person God created you to be.

Author's Note

Listen to advice and accept instruction,
that you may gain wisdom in the future.
Many are the plans in the mind of a man,
but it is the purpose of the LORD that will stand.

PROVERBS 19:20–21*

ongratulations! As you read this advice and accept this wisdom, you will be able to create sustainable financial freedom and independence. Many others and I have done it, and so can you! It is fun and enjoyable to take this exciting, money generating, mental journey into your tomorrows, starting with the thinking you are doing today.

I originally gave the material in this book as a talk in 1988 to thousands and thousands of mesmerized listeners in Huntington Beach, California. My glorious publisher, G&D Media, listened and heard the wisdom. They asked if I would update what I said, correct and modify

---

* Biblical quotations are taken from the English Standard Version unless noted otherwise.

anything that had changed, and turn it into this book. It was an irresistibly exciting idea. I instantly accepted the challenge.

As I have read and rewritten this transcription, I have again felt myself being loved, respected, and appreciated on that stage on that day. It was about an eight-hour talk, with a short lunch break. I am amazed and thankful to be able go back through the portal of time. I feel as if this all happened yesterday. It has reminded me of many things. My emotions, insights, ideas, illuminations, successes, and challenges, and the solutions that I have offered, have again filled my heart, mind, and soul with positive emotions. I am hoping they do the same, or more, for you.

It makes my heart happy that I can share these great ideas, which I believe will transform your life. My vision is that you will catch the essence of what happened on that day and that it will inspire you at the core of your being to be all you can be, do all you can do, and have all you can have. Happy reading!

Mark Victor Hansen
Scottsdale, Arizona
May 2021

For additional information on Mark's new books, audios, videos and seminars, please visit either markvictorhansen .com or hanseninstitute.com.

1

The Principles of Personal Achievement

Allow me to briefly share the backstory of why I am a lifelong student who will never stop studying wealth, riches, abundance and prosperity.

At nine years old, I desperately wanted a super-expensive European racing bicycle with low handlebars. The equivalent cost today would be about $4,000. My father owned a superb little Danish bakery, called Elite Bakery, with a cornucopia on the window design, so I assumed he could afford it. He could not. I knew he loved me, so I kept asking. He kept saying no.

Finally, I got an idea. I would ask him if I could have the bike if I earned it myself. He was sure that no nine-year-old could generate almost as much money as he was probably earning per year. He agreed, saying: "Pride of ownership always follows pride of earnership."

I intuitively knew the bike was mine if I could earn the money to pay for it. I looked up the word *earn* in Webster's dictionary, and it said that it meant *to supply labor or working services for pay.* I thought I could do that, although I did not have a clue about how.

I discovered that all we have to do is clearly and decisively know what we want and keep wanting it without distractions, and the *how* will manifest. Here is what happened to me then and hundreds of times since.

Miracle number one: I made pot holders and sold them to friends, neighbors, and relatives for 25 cents (back in 1957). Dad supplied all the raw materials for free, and I kept making and selling the pot holders and aggregating the quarters until I had enough to subscribe to a European bicycling magazine.

When the magazine arrived, I saw the bicycle of my dreams. I cut out the picture and taped it next to my bed. I was storyboarding before I even knew what storyboarding was. I looked at my future ideal racing bicycle every night longingly after praying, and fell asleep happily dreaming of riding my beautiful bicycle everywhere. In my mind, I was becoming what was called a Windy City Wheelman, cruising delightfully around all the enchanting back country roads.

Miracle number two: As a Boy Scout, I read every word of every issue of *Boys' Life* magazine. On the back page, I read an advertisement from Gibson Greeting Cards saying I could sell Christmas cards on consignment. I got a sample of the cards sent to me free, with order forms, and proceeded to sell. I took orders from my neighbors at $2 a box. I had my parents write a check for $1 per box, and I kept 50 percent, or $1 a box. The company sent the cards to me, and I had to personally deliver them to each buyer.

My mother was a great mom and a superstar storyteller and saleswoman. She taught me one line to say: "Hi, neighbor. I am Mark Hansen. I am earning my own bicycle selling Christmas cards. Would you like to invest in one box or two?" It went so well that I went around my block and kept making strides into new, ever expanding territories. I was relentless, happy, and unstoppable. I knew what I wanted and planned to get it. Working between 5:30 and 7 p.m. weeknights and Saturdays from 8 a.m. until 5 p.m., I sold 376 boxes in one month. I became the number one nine-year-old greeting card salesman in America and got the company's entrepreneurial award. Most importantly, *I earned my own money.*

Dad wisely took me to a bank to deposit my little first self-created fortune and gave me the bankbook to cherish. I was told to add to the account, because I had to save half my earnings for college someday. Hmm. This was not part of my immature plan, but yet another obstacle to overcome.

Miracle number three: Although I didn't even know it yet, my entrepreneurial journey was launched. My father's experience of suffering through the Depression, as he described it to my brothers and me, was not going to be my future experience. Intuitively I now knew I could sell and earn whatever I wanted.

I took jobs delivering the *Chicago Tribune* and *Sun-Times* newspapers mornings and nights. On Sundays, I cut lawns, washed windows, carried out garbage, cleaned out neighbors' garages, and did whatever I could get paid for that was honest, ethical, and beneficial. Suddenly, at the age of nine and three quarters, I had my own money. I did not share my mother's taste in clothes, so I bought my own clothes. I wanted to be cool, like Elvis Presley.

Miracle number four: I bought the bicycle and raced around a spherical track in Kenosha, Wisconsin, on Tuesday nights during the summer. However, I shone best in fifty-mile races, because my determination and persistence from peddling daily to deliver so many newspapers put me in inexhaustible shape for distance racing.

I share the above because it teaches the principles and philosophy of personal achievement:

1. Each of us has to start with a white-hot desire. You create ambitious desire and endlessly keep fanning it until you generate the result you want.

2. You can start with nothing but desire and can conquer every obstacle with imagination, persistence, and determination to succeed. You can become something in the process.

3. There is unlimited money waiting for *you* to take the initiative to act. No one can do your doing for you.
4. It all starts in your mind and imagination before it materializes and manifests.

Do you want more prosperity in your future than you've had in your past? Touch yourself on the chest and say, *I'm prosperous*. I wasn't always prosperous, but I've learned how to be. Here's what I believe, though, about gaining more prosperity: I believe you need to have fun all the time. When you work, you want to have fun. When you're home with the family, you want to have fun. Even when you're audited by the IRS, you want to have fun.

If you pay attention to what I have to share in this book, you will get the visit with the IRS. Most people go into an audit with apprehension, fear, doubt, as if they're going to have their house foreclosed on. The first time I was audited, the agent said, "Look at that: $40 a day for meals. How do you explain that?" I jokingly said, "I skip breakfast."

If you go in having fun, they won't know how to handle it. Not long ago, we came out of an audit. We feel so good about ourselves that we made the agent feel good about herself. In fact, she gave us an extra $2,000 back on top of what she planned on giving us.

You may be familiar with the classic self-help work by Maxwell Maltz: *Psycho-Cybernetics*. As it shows, the mind is teleological: whatever you set, you're going to get. Once I was in a program with my hero, comedian George Burns; he was ninety-two. People asked him how to live to be a hundred. "I'm booked into the Palladium on my hundredth birthday. They've prepaid me. I'm a Jewish gentleman, so I can't afford to die." He made it. He was born on January 20, 1896, and he died on March 9, 1996.

If you decide to become more prosperous than you are today, then you will. It is a guarantee. It is written in consciousness and in feeling before it is written in fact. What you think about comes about. If you change from unprosperous thinking to more prosperous thinking, you become more prosperous.

At some point, everybody gets rejected. Eventually even the best surgeon will have to bury a patient. Even the best attorney sooner or later loses a case. At some point, you, like me, will be rejected by somebody, and the more successful you get, the more critics you'll get. That's what stops a lot of people. It gives them the psychic whammy: "My God. What will they think?" My friend Terry Cole-Whittaker wrote a great book called *What You Think of Me Is None of My Business*. Eleanor Roosevelt said, "No one can reject me unless I give them my permission."

Nobody can step on your emotional butterfly unless you give them your permission. All of us start out as caterpillars. This book is set up to be the cocoon in which you can become a beautiful, high-flying butterfly—if you are ready.

Much of a lack of prosperity comes from self-rejection, so I'm going to get you out of self-rejecting and give you permission to be prosperous. Then I'm going to persuade you to become prosperous not only for yourself, but for total humankind, so you can be the highest, best, noblest, and most important world server. Whatever you're ready for is ready for you, so if you're ready for more prosperity, prosperity shows up. If you're ready for more love, more love shows up. If you're ready for more good, more good shows up. If you're ready for something awful to happen in your life, that's what you'll get. The law of expectation says you get what you expect, so you want to expect only unlimited good.

Use visuals to prepicture what you want as your prosperity future. You've got to have it before you get it. You might say that's gobbledygook, but you've got to have a notion of prosperity before you can become prosperous.

Also use affirmations. You grow into the words that you say to yourself, or that others say to you that you believe, think about, act upon, and then enact upon yourself.

In other words, prosperity starts with the idea. The idea is the one thing that takes nothing and turns it into something, and that's everything. If you've got great, grand, and terrific ideas, you get to have them, and they get to have you. There's an Olympics that happens first of all in the mind and then in your experience. You've got to impress it before you can express it. Before the rubber hits the road, you've got to have it in your mind.

You and I are here to manifest one thing, which is consciousness, awareness. When you change your awareness, you change your results. The apostle Paul said, "Be transformed by the renewal of your mind" (Romans 12:2). You have only your own mind and your own awareness. That's all you experience in this lifetime. You're living in your mind, which is your personal home entertainment center right now.

Right now, touch yourself and say aloud, *I'm ready*.

If you sit with any of the great people that have taken nothing and turned it into something, you'll find they've started with the one thing that's everything: the idea. They've also come through life with tremendous scar tissue, which enabled them to grow. On occasion, we'll have setbacks en route to our higher, loftier, nobler, and more inspired goal, and I'll teach you how to overcome them if you're ready.

By 1974, I'd been with the Leonardo da Vinci of our time, R. Buckminster Fuller. In his book *Nine Chains to the Moon*, Bucky (as he was called) restated Einstein's famous equation $E = MC^2$ so that a nine-year-old could understand that everything is energy in two forms, either radiance, like sunlight, or matter, that is, seemingly solid objects like a floor or a desk.

I'd met Bucky because I was doing some inventions and gave them to the board of Southern Illinois University. The head asked me, "Have you met Bucky Fuller?" and I said, "No." When I met him, I sat in his energy orbit, and I was absolutely wowed. I'd never had such a comprehensive expansion thinking experience before.

Bucky created synergetic mathematics, which holds that everything operates in triangulation, so when you want to build systems that work, they've got to have three elements—a trinity or triangulation. Every spiritual system has trinity; so do psychological systems and relationships.

Bucky used his mind more comprehensively than anyone I had ever met or experienced. Like him, I wanted to become a great and inspiring thinker, teacher, and leader.

In 1974, I was in New York City, and I was building geodesic domes, which Bucky had invented and patented. I was grossing $2 million a year. I was building the domes out of plastic called polyvinylchloride: PVC.

It was the time of the great oil crisis. The Arabs came up with an acronym of their own: OPEC. They said, "We can write checks so big your banks will bounce." That did me in. I crashed; I was bankrupt overnight and burned out. I went out to do day labor in Hicksville, Long Island, to unload toilet paper off a railroad car at the high fee of $2.14 an hour.

I arrived dressed in business attire: a trench coat and patent leather shoes. The boss said, "You don't look dressed right." I said, "I'm not staying long." Not that this wasn't good work for somebody, but it just wasn't the way I identified myself. Your prosperity comes out of your self-image, out of your self-I-am-age, which is why the affirmations we're going to use are I am statements, the nowness of life.

Today I can say that was my best worst experience. It's not bad if you go down. As I learned from Cavett Robert, the dean of professional speakers and founder of the National Speakers Association, it's only bad if you stay down, because if you're looking up, you will ultimately and inevitably go up. After my bankruptcy, I started learning and studying self-help material and decided to get into it.

The Bible says, "Draw near to God, and He will draw near to you" (James 4:8). Whatever idea you draw near to, whatever idea you put your attention on, you're going to get. If you put it on being healthy, you will become healthy. If you put it on being happy, you will become happy. You have ownership of this, and the only time you can do anything is *now*.

In Richard Bach's book *One*, he said, "In the exalted moment, there's an infinite potential of all alternative lives and lifestyles that you can live." That means if you start aiming for and claiming prosperity, then ultimately and inevitably you will start obtaining prosperity. It is an inside-outing rather than outside-inning.

Most of us say, "If it's prosperous around me, then I'll get prosperous." It couldn't be any more prosperous around you than it is right now (although it is going to be more so); you get to be prosperous at the level that you're ready for inside your mind.

You may say, "That's too easy." It is easy, but it's subtle. It is so subtle that most of us at some levels miss it. My friend, the late inspirational preacher Reverend Ike, used to say, "The best thing you can do for the poor is not be one of them." The only time you can be anything is *now*.

Muhammad Ali taught it to us most succinctly and colloquially, so no one missed it: "I am the greatest." As far as I'm concerned, there's nothing good about low ambition. It is a disservice to you, and it's a disservice to those around you. You need to have high, lofty, and inspired goals. If you have outrageous goals, you accomplish outrageous things. You need to activate your reticular activating mechanism, stimulate your medulla oblongata, and get your human biocomputer operating at its highest and best level.

Right now, say out loud, *I'm ready.*

In this book, I'm going to hit you with some material that you already know. I'm also going to hit you with material that will be brand-new, enlightening, enlivening, and enriching. Then I'm going to hit you with material that you may not even be able to apprehend, much less comprehend, much less use right now, but which you need to be ready for in the future.

I started doing prosperity talks in Midland, Texas, which is called the Oil Patch. Everybody in the room was worth between $10 million and $100 million. They asked me to talk about prosperity because they had made it as wildcatters, but they never had a consciousness around it. If you don't have a prosperity consciousness, you are susceptible to losing your money, as we've seen happen to a lot of people in the oil business. Because money goes where it is invited and stays where it is welcomed with a consciousness that accepts and cherishes it wisely.

In other words, as inspirational speaker Jim Rohn used to say, "If you get a million dollars, create in your mind a millionaire in consciousness, quick." It's true, because if you've got the money and you haven't got the consciousness of it, it'll slip through your fingers.

It's not good enough, in my estimation, just to have a lot of money. Many people are financially well off but are destitute as emotional human beings. They're missing the fact that what Og Mandino, the author of *The Greatest Salesman in the World*, has taught: you're not a human being but a human becoming. You're meant to become more and more and better and more alive.

Another great inspirational writer and speaker, the late Dr. Wayne Dyer, would say, "You're supposed to be a fully functioning, self-actualizing, no-limit human being," which both he and I learned from Dr. Abraham Maslow, the father of modern positive self-image psychology. At your best, you're unlimited.

Right now, touch yourself and say, *I'm unlimited.*

All of us have grown up with limitation. We've been told that we're too fat, too tall, too short, too ugly, too dumb, too stupid. All of that is irrelevant. It doesn't affect you unless you buy into it and believe it, consciously or subconsciously.

Wayne Dyer has a great story about a lady who came in to him for therapy and said, "My husband keeps telling me I'm stupid." Wayne said, "If your husband told you you were an automobile, would you open your mouth and get fuel?"

The point is to be a holistic, fully functioning human being, so you're completely prosperous at every level. You've got high-level wellness.

The question is, how much aliveness can you feel and how long can you feel it? Author Dr. Richard Moss talks not only about aliveness but about radical aliveness, where every cell of you is tuned in.

There are people who are totally blind. Even though they may not have physical sight, they've got the insight to catch prosperity.

Tom Sullivan lost his sight early in his life. He was born prematurely and was given too much oxygen in an incubator. He never condemned the nurse who did it and decided to be a fully functioning human being, participating in many sports. He said, "There's only one sport I can't play, and that's tennis." He wrestled for the United States in the 1968 Olympics. He was three seconds from getting pinned by his Russian opponent. He didn't want to lose, so he popped out one of his glass eyes. He said, "Oh my God. I lost an eye," which startled the Russian, and Tom won. He told his story in a book, *If You Could See What I Hear*, which was turned into an important inspirational film.

One of Tom's goals was to meet Arnold Palmer. When he did, he shook Arnold's hand and said, "I've always wanted to meet you. I've really wanted to be with you. As a matter of fact, Arnie, I want to golf with you."

Arnie said, "I'd like to golf with you, but I've never golfed with anyone blind."

Tom said, "I've got to tell you, Arnie, I'm a better golfer than you are. I'll bet you $1,000 a hole that I can whip you."

Arnie says, "My dear boy, I do this vocationally and avocationally. Word on the street is that I'm quite good. I can't take your $1,000 a hole. It would be too much."

Tom kept pressing and pressing. Arnie finally broke down and said, "OK. Anytime, anywhere."

"Tonight at midnight," said Tom.

Tom Sullivan and I were once together in Warren, Michigan. He walked into an environment, put out his hands, and said, "This place is tremendously opulent and prosperous, isn't it?" While he doesn't have the gift of physical sight, everything radiates. Every color we wear, every thought we think, our whole lifestyle is created as an atmosphere with energy and an aura around it. That's why Pierre Teilhard de Chardin, the French Jesuit priest, scientist, paleontologist, theologian, and philosopher, said, "The greatest expression of God in human form is the countenance of joy at a human face." The countenance of energy in any and all environments can be felt easily and immediately by sensitive blind people like Tom Sullivan. Intuitively, you could feel the emanations of another person.

Once we could only take X-rays internally, but today, with Kirlian photography, developed in Russia, we can photograph people's external metabolism. In the 1970s, the late Dr. Thelma Moss studied Kirlian photography at UCLA's Neuropsychiatric Institute, She could take a picture of your energy orb, your etheric energy, which is totally predetermined by your interior state of mind. This goes along with what Christ said: "The kingdom of God is within you" (Luke 17:21, King James Version).

The kingdom of God, or the kingdom of heaven, is our kingdom of conception. You are made in the image and likeness of God (Genesis 1:26), so you are here for three C's: to create, contribute, and be charitable. If you have a rich mental inner kingdom, then you become rich.

What else did Christ say? He said, "But seek first the kingdom of God, and his righteousness"—seek first the conception, seek first the awareness, seek first the consciousness—"and all these things shall be added to you" (Matthew 6:33).

Christ also said, "You always have the poor with you" (Mark 14:7). Why? Because they have a poor state of mind, which creates a poor state of result. Prosperity and poverty are both self-generated. I have self-generated myself out of poverty and into everlasting prosperity. I have taught millions of people around the world live to take ownership of their minds, awareness, and consciousness in order to end poverty. Poverty is a mental disease. Poverty belongs in one place only—a museum.

I'm part of the Hunger Project in a big way because I think it is imperative that we feed all of humanity. I've worked with the late Wayne Dyer and the late John Denver. Those of us that are plugged in at that level say, "Look, it is immoral to be able to grow food and pay farmers not to farm while we have starving people." Mahatma Gandhi wisely stated, "There is enough for everyone's need, but not for everyone's greed."

Proportionately, we're doing better in the world now than ever before. We have to keep making it better and better until 100 percent of humanity is economically and physically successful. That is my dedication and destiny. I will help to inspire a world that works comprehensively for all its inhabitants—macroprosperity for all. In 1900, 100 percent of the people in the world's 170 countries had somebody, or lots of somebodies, that were hungry. Today only 8.9 percent of humanity is starving.

Our goal: to feed all of humanity. How? By changing context. The old theory was trickle-down economics: give money to the rich, and it'll flow down throughout the economy. We've discovered that trickle-down doesn't cut it. The old-time politicians took people's money for themselves. They had the consciousness of thieves. We're using trickle-up economic theory, where we give people a few chickens and a few cows, and suddenly the whole community starts to feel the effects of prosperity. It's free enterprise at its best, where everyone can prosper and succeed, based on their own self-initiative to action. Incentivized individuals are positively self-determining and generate phenomenal wealth, riches, and prosperity.

We're in a brand-new consciousness, and we can't blame our predecessors: they didn't have what you and I have. We've got all of this new computerization, transportation, communication, the Internet, artificial intelligence, Zoom broadcasting, podcasting, and more. It has all happened within our lifetimes.

My dad came to this country from Denmark with the basic skills of a baker. Because America is, was, and always will be the land of opportunity, he prospered with a little bakery in Waukegan, Illinois. America is the cornucopia of greater good, the place where anything is possible, where you can go from rags to riches because freedom, free enterprise, and prosperity are encouraged and praised, and exalted.

My dad used to tell my brothers and me about one of his peers on the ship he came over on. Boats were only supposed to take seven to nine days coming over, depending on whether they hit bad weather. Unfortunately, the boat he was coming on, the *Gripsholm*, hit severe weather. It hit what are called seaquakes. The passengers experienced things like those you see in movies such as *The Poseidon Adventure*. For fifteen days, storms vectored this boat from port to port.

There was a Danish guy in steerage, who only brought enough food for nine days. By the twelfth day, he was really hungry. On the thirteenth day, he finally went up to the captain and said, "I'm starving, and if this lasts much longer, I'm not going to make it unless I get some food. Look, I'm an honest Danish guy, and if you would just feed me, I promise when I get to New York, I'll earn money and I'll pay you back."

The captain was astounded. He said, "My dear friend, when you paid for steerage, you also paid for the buffet on this boat. All the meals are included."

Understand from this story that when you and I entered onto Spaceship Earth, all the meals were included (even though you may have come through some parents that weren't into prosperity). Isn't that what Christ said? "I have come that [you] might have life, and have it more abundantly" (John 10:10). God was never into have-not-ness. The truth of truths is that God only knows and has created fundamental and endless supply.

Yet everybody has been told that spiritually you shouldn't get rich, because Christ was a poor carpenter (which he was not), and you're supposed to imitate that. Poverty came out of the Middle Ages, when the kings, nobles, and knights at the top of the pyramid were takers. They put a psychic whammy on the people under them, who were owned by and obligated to the monarchs.

I want you to understand that poorness has absolutely no virtue or value; it causes endless misery. In poverty you cannot manifest or express your highest and best self. You cannot serve greatly and find the fullness of your destiny. Poverty is an imprisonment of the worst kind. I know, because I experienced it when I was bankrupt. My tongue stuck to the roof of my mouth from living primarily on peanut butter. But I also understand that poverty is totally curable with right thinking, desires, and action in the right, prosperous direction.

The more we have, the more we have to give. America is the greatest nation because we're the most giving nation in the world. We've got it, so we can give it. We give more than the 170 other countries around the world combined.

Right now, jab yourself in the chest with two fingers and say, I'm *abundant*, and *I'm getting into more abundance*.

Again, what you think about comes about. If you plan on more abundance, you'll find more.

You've got to be careful, because some theories are going around right now that I want to debunk. One is that if you have less, somebody else can have more. That is absolute poppycock and insanely stupid. I'll give you many examples that show the idiocy of that.

The second myth is that we're going to have a recession or a full-blown depression in a very short time. The only way that will happen is if people lock onto fear and stop trading and doing commerce nationally and internationally, as they did in 1929. We've just come through a Covid-19 lockdown. What have we seen happen? Not only has the market done well, but skyrocketingly well: a lot of people are saying the Dow will go to 40,000 and maybe all the way up to 50,000 in a very short time. We are in prosperous times, and as long as we think prosperous, we will stay prosperous.

Prosperity is achieved at one level only: individually. Whatever the individual mind does reflects, ricochets, and goes into the corporate, political, and global mind. When I went bankrupt back in the seventies, the mayor in New York was Abe Beame, and he was not a prosperity thinker. I would say—if you don't mind the pun—he was off the beam. He kept saying, "New York's going bankrupt. New York's going bankrupt." One gets what one conceives, believes, affirms, and executes. As a leader, Mayor Beame was repetitively polluting the minds of his constituents, because whatever is frequently repeated and believed ultimately becomes the belief of the followers.

What did the businesses do? They went to Connecticut. They went to New Jersey. They went to Florida. They split, and New York's prices started to plummet. Into the mayoral office comes a guy named Ed Koch, who believed that New York was booming and kept saying so with feeling and belief, and voilà! All of a sudden New York was booming.

Your state of mind creates your state of result. That's why Christ said, "To the one who has, more will be given, and he will have an abundance" (Matthew 13:12). Haveness is a state of mind before you have the state of experience.

Christ added, "From the one who has not, even what he has will be taken away." The good news is you can change at any time if you are ready.

Right now, tell yourself out loud, *I am ready.*

The late Bob Hope is one of my heroes. He was the greatest individual philanthropic institution. He used to raise in excess of $1 billion a year for charities. I asked him, "Why do you work with all the churches, temples, synagogues, the USO, and every charity in America?"

He smiled and said, "That way I don't get kicked out of heaven on a technicality."

I saw Bob at tons of occasions, and I got to spend time with him, because that was one of my 101 written goals. Remember, it doesn't cost anything to write down your goals. You can write down anything. When you write it and believe it, you will achieve it.

Write down 101 goals. They will immediately start to show up in your experience. You'll synchronize in time and space with each and every goal that you really want and are persistently committed to experiencing. (Most people fail to truly answer the question: what do you want?) When you put your goals in writing, sooner or later, one way or another, inevitably, ultimately, it's got to show up. It's got to manifest. Faith that your goals will be accomplished precedes hope. Hope in turn sends a message that makes you feel good. High hope detoxifies you and gives you greater longevity and greater flexibility.

At the turn of the twentieth century, a minister and lawyer named Dr. Russell Conwell published one of the first self-help books, called *Acres of Diamonds*. It tells the story of a farmer in Africa who desperately wanted to find diamonds. He went to his priest and said, "Where are diamonds found?" The Priest answered, "Diamonds rise at the bottom of rushing streams."

The farmer sells his farms and spends his whole life trying to find diamonds, never having any success. Finally he returns to visit his original farm before he dies. He looks at the mantelpiece, and on it there's a stone that ultimately turns to be a 576-carat diamond.

The farmer sees this diamond because he finally knows what he's looking for. He asks the guy who bought the farm, "Where did you find that?"

"In the backyard. There's tons of them."

The farmer was on top of the Kimberley Mine and never knew it. What he was looking for had always been immediately before him.

Likewise, our real wealth starts inside our mind. It is said to be closer than our breath and nearer than our hands or feet.

Conwell gave his "Acres of Diamonds" talk six thousand times—the most repeats of the same talk ever at that time. He earned $7 million and founded the great Temple University. Conwell came out of nothing and went on to create Temple University, and the rest became history. He is one of the people that I would hold up as having mastered prosperity, and his legacy has taught it to millions of students.

What did Conwell do? He got a new vision. Today each of us needs a new vision. Solomon, the richest man in history, said, "Where there is no vision, the people perish"

(Proverbs 29:18, King James Version). I have transmuted that to say, "With vision, I flourish."

Right now, touch yourself and say, *With vision, I flourish and flourish, making everybody better off and nobody worse off.*

If you haven't visited William Randolph Hearst's phenomenal estate, called San Simeon, in California, please put it on your bucket list. It will inspire your potential wealth building ideas—as will Andrew Carnegie's home at Fifth Avenue and 92nd Street in New York City. Liberace, the flamboyant and accomplished pianist, created the Liberace Museum Collection in Las Vegas, using the money it generated to fund music scholarships for deserving kids.

What am I saying? I want you to learn how to earn all that you possibly can. I want you to learn how to save all that you can. Invest all that you can. Leave a money generating legacy that serves in a direction that you have predetermined will be omnibeneficial. Decide now to give all you possibly can in unique, honorable, and lasting ways.

2

The Richest Man in Babylon

In 1926, George Clason published a great book called *The Richest Man in Babylon*. It wisely says, "Part of all you earn is yours to keep. Save the first 10 percent."

Tithing also works. I wrote a book called *The Miracle of Tithing*. I teach that there are four T's to tithing: tithe your thinking, your time, your talent, and your treasure. Once you have done that, abundantly add a fifth T: be thankful. The Mormons have created powerful amounts of wealth because they teach and practice tithing.

You've got to live in principle if you want to succeed. Principles never wear out, rust out, get tired, or go on holiday. Like gravity, they simply keep working.

It's very simple. I repeat: I want you to earn all you can, save all you can, invest all you can, and invest wisely with prudence, with people that have proven track records.

Christ said: "You will know them by their fruits"—meaning by their results, accomplishments, achievements, records, and history.

If somebody's going to say, "I want to take your money and make it multiply," you say, "Great. I would love you to take my money and make me richer. Show me your financial statement, and show me how much money you've made and have in this investment." Don't put any money where somebody else hasn't been putting their money. Don't play with anyone who hasn't already won in that game. Let somebody else break their pick and learn the program. Prospectors usually were losers. If you read Napoleon Hill's *Think and Grow Rich*, which is one of the mandatory books in my prosperity teaching, you will see "Three Feet from Gold" as a chapter title. It is important to know where the gold is and who finishes the job of finding and mining it.

Here's a fact: you can start with nothing but a white-hot, burning desire, and make it as big as you want. I want you to earn all you can, save all you can, invest all you can, and then be as philanthropic as you can. Let your charitable tendencies out. Be a magnificent, magnanimous giver.

You may say, "I've got nothing to give." If you've got a smile, an encouraging word, praise, or a push to someone else in the right direction, you've got something important to give. You never know: the person you smile at may be ready to commit suicide and may have said, "If one person smiles at me, I won't die."

My coauthor Jack Canfield tells a great story about a guy who said, "I'm going to walk nineteen miles from my house to the Golden Gate Bridge. If one person smiles at me on the way, I won't commit suicide. To make sure somebody remembers that I said that, I'll write a note and leave it on my door, and the postman will see it tomorrow." The guy got all the way to the Golden Gate Bridge and not one person had smiled at him.

That's all that he required. One smile. Is that so much? It's free. It takes fewer muscles to smile than to frown. I want you to smile even if the teeth aren't yours. I want you to develop twinkle wrinkles in your face. I want you to feel so good about yourself that you smile all the time. It will make the world around you brighter, happier, and much more abundant.

Wayne Dyer said, "If you crush an orange, the only thing that can come out is orange juice. If somebody aggravates you, the only thing that can come out of you is anger, but you put the anger in there first. That's why it comes out."

Wayne was once in a grocery store down in Florida. A guy jammed a stick in his back, and Wayne turned around. He was always in tremendous physical shape. He was ready to deck the guy but then saw he had a white cane. Immediately Wayne released his anger and said,

"I'll help you through the line first. I didn't see that you were behind me. My apologies."

When you come up to life's golden ticket counter, you have to know whether you want to be prosperous or unprosperous. Life doesn't care. Life is neutral. That's why Christ says that God "makes his sun rise on the evil and on the good, and sends rain on the just and on the unjust." (Matthew 5:45). The subconscious is neutral. It also reasons deductively. It goes from the general to the specific. If you program the mind to get rich, you will become rich.

And the good news here is, as happy as you are, you can be happier. As healthy as you are, you can be healthier. As loving as you are, you can be even more loving. As rich as you are, you can be even richer.

Your mind and your right thinking can be your ticket to anywhere, and the ticket to anywhere starts at different levels for all of us. You can decide to have self-replenishing prosperity: it may be a car, it may be a house, it may be new clothes, money in a bank account, paying off your debts, the vacation that you've always dreamed of taking.

I want you to have perfect self-expression. I want you to have the right livelihood. It's obvious to me that I wasn't in my right livelihood back when I went bankrupt, so I didn't know that you could have continuing growth, expression, total economic security, and ever increasing freedom. I didn't know how to live a principle-centered life. Experience and practice principle-centered leadership, where you're creating and self-managing yourself to the highest and best.

Dr. Steve Covey, author of *The Seven Habits of Highly Successful People*, says that in order to succeed, you've got to communicate your vision, but before you can communicate your vision, first of all, you have to have one.

Right now, jab yourself in the chest and say, *I'm getting my vision.* Even do a plural: *I'm getting my visions.*

I teach people to write down at least 101 goals because the spiritual man wakes up the secular man at the level of desire, and I'm here to stab your spirit alive. It is incredible what can be done.

My father had the vision to come to America. When he arrived for the first time in 1921, he went through immigration at Ellis Island. Although he only had an eighth-grade education in the baker's trade, he was really a great culinary artist. He always joked that he liked playing with the dough.

To get his citizenship, my father had to answer sixty oral examination questions in front of a federal court judge, letter-perfect. At the end, the examiner put out his meaty hands and said, "Congratulations, Mr. Hansen. You're now an American. Can I ask you one perfunctory question?"

My dad said, "Judge, if I'm an American, you can ask me anything you want, but I don't know what a perfunctory is."

"What are the last two words of the national anthem?"

My dad said, "That's easy. Play ball."

Today I want to play ball with your mind, but I don't want to just hit a home run. I want to hit a grand slam home run. Understand this: each one of us who wakes up makes everybody better off. You are here to become a record setter and a history maker. You are God's greatest miracle. You are to live up to the best that is in you and inspire others to do the same or more.

I want you to get this message to as many other people as you can, because one of the basic principles of prosperity is: each one, teach one. In the eighteenth century, Lawrence Tribble wrote:

One mind awake,

Awakens another.

The second awakens

His next door brother.

The three awake can rouse a town

By turning

the whole place

Upside down.

The many awake

Can cause such a fuss

It finally awakens the rest of us.

One man up,
With dawn in his eyes
Surely then
Multiplies

If you want more prosperity, teach what you most need to learn. As author Dr. Jean Houston says, it "creates for you a walkwoom." She tells the story of getting her first PhD at Harvard under the great theologian Dr. Paul Tillich. For three days, he kept saying with his German accent that if you want to succeed, you have to understand the "walkwoom." Being the youngest PhD candidate at Harvard, she timidly raised her hand and said, "Professor Tillich, would you be so kind as to write 'walkwoom' on the board, please? I looked it up, and I can't find it in German or in English. I've asked the class members, and they don't know what you mean either."

He wrote, "To succeed, you must have a *vacuum*."

I want to make your mind a low-pressure zone. Meteorologically, wind does not blow on the earth. It is actually sucked into a low-pressure zone. I want you to create a vacuum in your mind and inner being by saying, "I'm attractive to wealth." All of a sudden, it'll just show up. All the right people, all the right events, all the right experiences will show up right here and right now, for the simple reason that you're ready. You may ask, it's that easy? Yes—you're ready, you give yourself permission, and suddenly you start accepting prosperity. You don't have to be any one particular way.

How do I know this? Because I get three hundred letters or more from people every week. One lady wrote that somehow all my books and tapes ended up at Goodwill. She got to buy all of them for a very reduced rate. She said, "I always worked for somebody else as a seamstress. Then I read your book *Future Diary* and listened to your tapes. I created a new self-image for myself. I now own a little business, and I've already got three assistants. All that has happened in six months."

Transformation doesn't take long. If it did, you couldn't have a guy like Bill Gates become a billionaire at less than age twenty-nine.

When I was a little kid, it was a big deal to be a millionaire. Now in America, we have one million millionaires, and almost three thousand billionaires. *Forbes* magazine says that America during Covid-19 has been creating over one billionaire a day. I learned a great line from Rev. Ike, "Don't curse the rich, or you won't be one of us." Concentrate on the people that are doing the best with their prosperity. Communicate a vision.

3

Clarify Your Purpose

Next, clarify your purpose. If you don't have a purpose, your purpose is to get one. In 1961, aerospace engineer Wernher von Braun stimulated President Kennedy's imagination, saying, "You know, it is possible to land a man on the moon. We have to beat the Russians with their new Sputnik in space and win the space race." The next day, President Kennedy got in front of the American public and said, "In this decade we will land a man safely on the moon."

Von Braun came back to the Oval Office and said, "Mr. President, what are you doing? Are you crazy? That was science fiction I was talking about. I don't know if we can make it science fact."

President Kennedy said, "Good. Do it in a decade."

That's why I want you to have a big purpose. Big purposes have a lot of juice. The Bible says that God's ways are "past finding out" (Romans 11:33, King James Version). God knows how to do everything; landing on the moon and conquering space was part of his plan.

Given a giant challenge, Von Braun found the resources and delivered the moon landing and return in less than a decade. All the resources of the universe show up to do to your bidding, because God only knows how to say yes.

You say, "Oh my God. I can't pay my bills. I can't do it. I don't know how to do it. They're going to repossess my car, shut off my telephone, take back my credit cards."

God only says yes. Whereas if you've seen all your bills paid off and you say, "I'm cutting it. I'm doing marvelously. Everything is in flow. All the right people are showing up in my life. I've got the right associates, the right assistants, the right Master Mind partners. I'm doing bidding that I never thought possible. I'm beyond my wildest expectations."

Again, God only knows how to say yes. I'm here to help you turn on your dream machine. Pretend you've got a knob in your neck. Say, *I'm turning on my dream machine*, and turn it on.

Then don't let anyone turn off your dream machine.

Get some new dreams. Declare them, and make sure they're bold.

Motivational speaker Earl Nightingale and I once toured all of Australia, and we argued every day on the media, because that's the way we got lots of people to show up—thousands and tens of thousands. Earl argued that you shouldn't tell your goals to anyone: let your results do your bidding. That is one way to do it.

I say, "Find a group that is like-minded." Now it's critical to understand those last two words. To get prosperity, you've got to have a like-minded group, a Master Mind support team, people who see more in you than you see in yourself. Two together have the power of eleven: 1 + 1 = 11.

Avoid hanging around people that keep seeing you as the way you currently are. That's why, more often than not, mothers and fathers hit our hot buttons: because they remember how we were when we were kids and they haven't seen our evolution. They haven't understood our transformation. They are still locked into the thought of where we were.

When people come to hear me now, after having heard me ten or fifteen years ago, they say, "My God, have you changed! I didn't want to come back." I don't blame you. Fifteen years ago, I wasn't who I am now.

You aren't the same person you were years ago. Every seven years, you're going through metamorphosis. Peter Drucker, the management guru, says, "Change what you do or how you do it once every seven years, just to stay full of aliveness." Write a purpose and make sure the purpose is big.

I'm here to make a positive difference in your life. Helen Keller said, "My candle lit yours. You light yours on mine. It didn't take anything from mine. It makes the world fourfold brighter."

That's the law that I learned from Bucky Fuller, and which I will teach in this book. It's called *synergy*, the behavior of whole systems, which cannot be predicted by the functions of their separate parts.

We're in this wonderful pregnant time in history, going into a century of phenomenal change, where for the first time we're communicating with all of humanity—eight billion people alive, and we can talk to anyone in nanoseconds. You can use your cell phone and talk live to someone half way around the world in India. You can select a picture on your phone, press *send*, and immediately they are looking at it.

We're in the age of speedup, and we're in the speedup of learning. Anything that's knowable is knowable by all of humanity. This is why Ken Keyes wrote his famous book *The Hundredth Monkey*. It tells about some monkeys who live on islands off of Japan. The old monkeys ate dirty sweet potatoes, while some of the young monkeys went down to the water and washed their sweet potatoes. When the hundredth monkey caught the vision of eating cleanly washed and probably tastier sweet potatoes, suddenly all monkeys on the neighboring islands also got the telepathic message and started washing their sweet potatoes. It was telepathy, because there is an invisible communication circuit from monkey mind to monkey mind.

That's also what happens as we have breakthroughs in prosperity. Prosperity starts with one person. It always starts in the invisible and metamorphizes into the visible, transmuting into its physical counterpart. That's why Christ said, "But when you pray, go into your room and shut the door and pray to your Father who is in secret. And your Father who sees in secret will reward you." (Matthew 6:6). He's talking about the secret room of your mind. Lock the door; lock yourself in with the good and the final results that you truly want and desire.

You've got to see it in your mind before you can see it in your experience. It's 1974, and I'm with my Master Mind partner, Chip Collins. He asked me, "What do you really want?"

"Someday I'd like to be prosperous enough, amongst other things, to be chauffeur-driven in a luxury car to my own estate. I'd like the gate to close behind me. I'd like to buzz down a window. I'd like the olfactory nature of my environment to imbue my nostrils and fluff my aura."

I now own that place. At the time it was owned by my friend Dr. Jerry Parker, and I said, "This is my new home." He gave me a first, a second, and a third mortgage.

We have night-blooming jasmines on the side. We've got pine trees in the land of palm trees because I like that smell at night. We've got gardenias trellising up our staircase. We have ornamental horticulturists who made our environment gorgeous, with my wife's help. We have fresh edibles on a daily basis. We live in Southern California, where we have fresh strawberries year-round, and kumquats, so my three-year-old daughter could say, "Pick me up, daddy, so I can harvest a kumquat." We can pick fresh avocados.

Why not? Why not see how much life force energy you can have access to? The only closed system in the universe is the universe, and Einstein said, "The universe is finite but boundless."

It is the only self-perpetuating, never-ending system. Any other system cannot be self-perpetuating. That makes you an open system, but if you're an open system, why not decide in favor of yourself to take on the best?

Nothing could be better than cutting your own fresh fruit and fresh vegetables and eating them. I really believe in organic gardening. As Dick Gregory said in his little book *Mother Nature's Cooking Real Good*, "The closer you can get to the vine, the more life force energy you're going to get, and it will be divine." You pick a fresh apple. Even though you know that it has not been sprayed with pesticide, you still rub it on your shirt, and you bite into it. It snaps; it's supertasty and full of revitalizing energy.

When you bite into a strawberry and the juice is so succulent that you can't believe that you've been the one watering it, you are into heightened prosperity. You know that you are feeding your nutritional system the best that exists.

I'm not berating the big food companies. But even they would say, if you can grow it, harvest it, and eat it at its peak, you will be infinitely healthier, with a stronger immune system, and your body will be more satisfied and not crave junk food.

If you're going for prosperity, make your behavior congruent with your belief. Here's the deal. The middle three letters of the word *believe* are *lie*. That means that if you don't believe you're prosperous, if you start denying what you've been affirming, you'll talk yourself out of it. My cliché is, 1 percent doubt, and you're out. You can't say, "Maybe I'm rich. Maybe I'm successful." Either you are or you aren't. You have the state of mind before you get the result.

Remember, when you put it out, it comes back, and in strange and wonderful and delicious forms. The minute you put it out into the universe, somebody's going to come in and hit you with an idea. If you are not in the right space, you could take it as an attack. If you're in the right space, you can say, "I'll add it on and I'll make it better." The Japanese started out making junk, and made it into manufacturing the highest quality, all by a transformation of consciousness.

Christopher Columbus tried for years to sell people on the idea of sailing across the Atlantic to reach new territory, but their belief system was out of whack. It's not many years ago that people believed that the earth was totally flat and that you could sail off the end of it, or you'd meet with the dragons. He finally convinced Queen Isabella of Spain, and she talked her husband, Ferdinand, into hawking the crown jewels to underwrite this trip.

Columbus got several ships to roll out. History books tell us thirty-nine of his crew members wanted to mutiny and told him to turn around. To them he said, "You can swim home."

See, 1 percent doubt, you're out. He couldn't back up. Christopher Columbus sails out and comes back. Isabella and Ferdinand pull out all the stops. They invite all the monarchs to herald their great achievement, getting to what they thought was the Indies.

As I've said that when you become successful, you are guaranteed to get critics, but as Zig Ziglar said, "They don't make statues to critics." The story of the haves and have-nots is the story of the dids and did nots. That's why Emerson said, "Do the thing, and you'll have the power."

Anyway, a courtier of the Spanish court comes up and says to Columbus, "Anybody could have done that." Columbus did not get uptight. He had good self-esteem. He'd earned the right. (When you get prosperous, you've earned the right to talk about prosperity.) Columbus calls over a white-gloved maître d' at this hoedown, and says, "Bring me a hard-boiled egg." He hands the hard-boiled egg to the courtier and says, "If you're so smart, make the egg stand on end for twenty minutes."

The courtier tries, and it topples over fruitlessly. They head up and down the head dais. No one can make the egg stand on end. Columbus takes it, smashes it down, and dents it. It now stands up. He says, "Now that I've shown you how, it's easy."

In this book, I will show you how to become prosperous and it will become easy. Isn't that what Abe Maslow taught us about self-actualizing human beings? You start out unconsciously incompetent. You don't know that you don't know, and you don't care. At age three, you become a conscious incompetent: Mom tells you, "Look, kiddo, Mom wants you to learn to tie your shoes." You become a conscious competent. You can now tie the shoes. You get so good and it becomes so regular that you can tie them without looking. You become an unconscious competent. It becomes effortless effort.

Your goal is to make prosperity effortless effort.

4

Contacting Infinite Intelligence

Think about the amount of money you spend on your automobile on a monthly basis—probably hundreds of dollars at least. The same on your clothes, or even on your hair.

Aren't you worth a little bit more to know how to feel good about yourself and how to control the one thing that *is* everything and gives you anything you want—which is your mind?

We've got more information than ever before. We're getting information overload. It seems to me there's only one hope for all of us: we've got to intuitively ask our inner knower.

Everyone's got one. Sometimes we pollute it by saying, "I don't know," but your inner knower knows. All of us have the ability to go into what in India they call the *akashic record*. Napoleon Hill called it infinite intelligence. Teilhard de Chardin called it the noösphere. The spiritually minded call it God. It doesn't matter what you call it. That infinite, inner intelligence knows, and it knows that it knows that it knows, and it can only tell you the truth.

When you know the truth, the truth will set you free. Your inner knower says, "I do want this" or "I don't want this." It's just like speed-reading a book: before you start, you tell yourself, "I'm going to pick out the material I need in the nowness of my consciousness. All the rest is there for me at a later time if I want to savor it and digest it mentally, but right now this is what I need, and I'll pick it up."

When I went bankrupt, I was ready to slash my wrists. As I say in my book *Dare to Win*, "When your self-worth goes up, your net worth automatically and axiomatically goes up." I thought self-worth and net worth were the same. When my net worth went down, I thought I had zero self-worth, so I wanted to slash my wrist.

I never listened to inspirational audios. I was too good. I was too sophomoric. I knew too much. Luckily, I was given an audio by Cavett Robert called *Are You the Cause or Are You the Effect?* He said, "Are you the creature of circumstance or the creator?"

If I'm the creator, I created this bankruptcy, which I did; I can see that with hindsight. I couldn't see it when

I was going through it. Many of the problems you go through are going to be your best worst experiences. You can't see why you're going through them, except with hindsight, which gives you insight, which is going to be out of sight.

Anyhow, I listened to that one audio. I had a tape player in my beat-up old Volkswagen. I was driving around, listening to one tape 287 times and checking it off every time I listened to it. Cavett said, "If you look up, you go up." I thought, "Wow, that's hot." I kept saying to myself, "Cavett's saving my life. Someday, if I ever get to serve him some way, I want to do it."

At one point, Cavett's daughter Lee called me up and said, "Daddy just had a third heart attack. He's in a heap of hurt, and he'd like you to call him right now."

I said, "I'd do anything for your daddy. He saved my life."

When I called Cavett, he said, "Would you fill in for these engagements that I can't make? I'm going to be in a holding pattern in the hospital a little longer than I thought." He thought that when he was going into the hospital that time, it would be like brushing your teeth or going to the dentist and coming right out, ready to go back on the platform without missing a beat. I was happy to oblige.

Cavett Robert taught me that each of us is going to spend over five years of our lives in a car. Cavett's suggestion to me was make your driving time learning time. Get a little classroom on wheels, by listening full-time to inspirational, educational, and motivational audios. If you're emotionally down, it gets you up. If you're up, it gets you higher.

The best time to listen to inspirational material is in the morning, when you're driving to work, because you wake up in a hypnopompic state of trance. When you go to sleep, you're in a hypnagogic trance. Those are the two times when consciousness is most malleable, moldable, and transformable.

I'm addicted to listening to audios. My car is loaded with other people's audios. I also share great audios with all my best friends because I believe in sharing these insights, this wisdom, and these wow ideas.

Some of us find it unpleasant to tone their bodies and exercise. I like to listen to audios while I exercise. I like having sweat pour out of me. I get two benefits simultaneously: I learn and get fit. While learning, I don't even recognize the stress, struggle, or pain of exercise.

Audios can take you into profound and sometimes transcendent levels of thinking. I don't know anyone that really likes getting into high-volume sit-ups, but if you're listening to audios, it doesn't bother you.

Exercise your mind. Have a PMA (positive mental attitude). Get a private tutor—and audios are the best private tutors. They are relatively inexpensive, last forever, can be shared with your Master Mind partners, and can be turned on whenever you want to listen and learn. Earl Nightingale once said to me, "Audio recordings are more important than the Gutenberg press, for the simple reason that right now, out of all of humanity, only 50 percent can read, but 100 percent, barring the hearing-impaired, can listen."

After you finish listening to an audio or reading a book, if you know somebody that's hungry or thirsty to grow and be a little bit more motivated, my request to you is share your audios and books. I know some of my peers don't want that. They keep emphasizing, "This is copyrighted material." They act as if God will strike your head with a bolt of lightning. I have a different point of view: you get to share this material. That's why I record my audios in front of live, terrific audiences.

Cavett also said that to be positive, you've got to do spaced repetition learning, where you go over and over what you need to learn. Little kids are the best at this. To learn things, you repeat them again and again.

When my daughters were little, I would read two hours a night to them, and their favorite book to finish with was *The Little Engine That Could*: "I think I can, I think I can, I think I can, and then I'll say I did." We went over this book hundreds of times.

You learn it, or you lose it. Sixty-four percent of what you hear today is gone in twenty-four hours: 98 percent is gone in a week. According to Dr. Maxwell Maltz, author of *Psycho-Cybernetics*, the only way to learn is to go over the same idea seventeen to twenty-one times.

Sometimes you want to share material like this with a spouse that is not so happy or positive or with irascible teenagers, rather than somebody who's as avant-garde and together as you are. Once in a while in regular audiences, I have some spouse hit another in the ribs and say, "Bam. He hit us. He's talking to you," or they go home with the audios and say, "I just heard this guy. Now you listen to him." That is not the program. Do it with finesse, please. Drive around in your car and plunk in one of the audios. They'll start laughing. They'll start getting it.

I wish you could read the letters I get from teenagers. One recent letter said, "Until I listened to you, I thought I was a pimple."

During one program I did in Las Vegas, a mother came up to me with tears in her eyes and asked, "Did you watch a movie on teenage suicide?"

"Yes, ma'am," I said.

"You know, I watched that."

"Ask your kid if he ever contemplated suicide," I told her.

When the program was over, I asked the mother, "Did you ask?" Because I knew the answer. I thought in advance, "The kid's good looking, en route to college, and got a glorious girlfriend."

He had told her, "Yeah, mom, on five occasions." His best friend had snuffed out his life three weeks earlier. She asked him, "Why didn't you?"

He said, "You had me read Mark's book *Future Diary*, which said that you've got to be afraid to die until you have contributed something great to humanity, and I haven't made my contribution yet."

I ask people to take copies of *Future Diary* home for their teenagers, because kids commit suicide when they don't have purpose or meaning. Nobody taught them how to make life successful and fulfilling or how to set goals and become rich.

5

The Pygmalion Effect

Here's the deal on prosperity. Romans 11:33 says that God's ways are past finding out. He's talking about the God in you. Your mind already knows how to make you prosperous and how to do it right.

There was a myth in ancient Greece about a sculptor named Pygmalion. He made a statue of a woman that was so beautiful that he fell in love with it, and his love made the statue come alive.

The great playwrights George Bernard Shaw was inspired by this myth to write his famous play *Pygmalion*, which was later made into the musical *My Fair Lady*. In it Professor Higgins and his partner saw little Eliza Doolittle, took her into their laboratory for six weeks, and transformed her into an elegant lady who could pass for royalty, and no one could discern where she came from. She was fast-educated to go from rags to riches with class, dignity, distinction, savior faire, and panache.

This is the process that I'm talking about. Today in psychology, we call it the Pygmalion effect. You take yourself from where you are to where you want to be.

Here's a homework assignment for the next six weeks: every day, when you wake up, claim, "I'm rich, I'm abundant, I'm prosperous." Do it in a singsong. Get to your hopes, dreams, and future. The true joy in life is being used by a purpose recognized by yourself and everyone as a mighty one.

In this book, I'm doing everything I can to be a gadfly to your greater good. When you finish it, don't let yourself go back into the same habit patterns. Think anew. Say out loud, "I'm thinking anew."

When you're thinking anew, you're writing into your own success the future book of your life, where you have the freedom to be it, do it, and have it.

Say, *I've got the freedom.*

I want to talk about freedom. My friends Naomi and Jim Rhode owned a $50 million dollar a year company called Semantodonics in Phoenix (later renamed Smart-Practice). At this time, they only trained dentists. They took hundreds of dentists and orthodontists over to China, where they all bicycled the whole Great Wall of China.

A few days later, Naomi was in a shop. There was a tall, elegant gentleman behind the counter, who was obviously Chinese. She innocently asked, "Have you seen the Great Wall of China?"

"No, I've never seen the Great Wall of China."

Naomi was astounded. This was a time before China opened up, when people got to work in one of two colors: blue and gray. She said, "Why haven't you seen the Great Wall?"

He said, "Well, here in China, we work twenty-nine days a month for twelve to fourteen hours a day. During my whole lifetime, I'm allowed only to go twenty-nine miles from my house."

He went on: "I speak eloquent English, and I've got the equivalent of an MBA here. But for the rest of my life, I will work in this store at a counter one foot wide and three feet long. This is my territory. This is my province."

"Do you have any dreams?"

"Yeah, I've got one."

"What's that?"

"I want to go to the United States of America."

"Why is that?"

"Because in the United States of America, you can be a success."

"How do you define that?"

"There, you can do what you want, when you want, with whoever you want, as much as you want."

In China, there is no real freedom. Freedom exists in America because our forefathers believed in free enterprise and established a constitution, and a rule of law by which to live. Be thankful for it. Appreciate it. Prosper by it. Use it to your and everyone else's benefit. Remember, it is a sacred trust and must be forever protected, guarded, cherished, and guaranteed. Those principles made America the greatest nation in the world, and we have to defend those hard-earned rights and privileges.

Abe Maslow spoke about cognitive being-values, which are holistic and accepting rather than deficient and judgmental. One of these, in my opinion, is mental freedom: you've got to be free in your mind.

For a second, close your eyes and feel yourself being free. We'll focus on the economic level because that's what we're talking about here. What is freedom for you? Is it just paying off your bills? Is it just having enough to eat? Is it $100,000, $1 million, $5 million, $10 million? Whatever *enough* is for you, just say to yourself, "I've got it right now, and I can feel it."

Go into the bank account called your imagination, and be there with all that abundance, all that joy, all those relationships. Know that all the relationships you've dreamt of creating are now yours. Just know that all is yours, and there's more coming. You may now open your eyes. Does that make you feel good? That's the kind of consciousness to get into. Do you feel a little bit more self-confident after buying into that kind of conscious-ness?

I want you to fully experience the joy of living, to cre-ate personal wealth and financial security for yourself and inspire others to do so too. It seems to me that if you're really living at your highest and best, you can inspire at least one person a month to get into doing whatever it is that you do. When I'm talking to chiropractors (or what-ever profession it is), I say, "If you're really doing a good job, I hope a lot of you get others to become chiropractors also."

Be a fully functioning, no-limit human being. Expe-rience personal fulfillment. Experience high self-esteem. Be a being of choice. Decide that life is great and that you're going to live it in the most abundant way possible. Self-esteem is the front end of your creation.

Using a scale of 1 to 10, where 10 is high and you're a fully functioning, no-limit person, George Gallup con-ducted a poll and discovered that most Americans feel like a 6 or less. Here's the problem with emotively feeling like a 6 or less: you only hang out, work, play, love, and marry people that are 5's, 4's, 3's, 2's, or 1's.

Your self-esteem determines how you live at a mate-rial level. The car you drive is a statement of your self-esteem, as are the house you live in, the way you keep your house, the clothes that you wear, and the people that you associate with. They are all externalizations of your internalized self-esteem, all of which is changeable when you are ready to change.

Spiritually, whatever you add to an *I am* statement, you become. Whatever you want to change, start with changing *I am* with feeling and belief. The words you add to *I am* become your life's directional compass. Your inner *I am* is like a GPS to your mind, brain and heart.

Right now, say *I am* aloud, and add to it whatever you want to be or become. When we're tuning ourselves up for prosperity, the first line is, *I am creating self-replenishing prosperity in my life.*

I suggest that you write these words on a 3 x 5 card, wrap a $100 bill around it, and carry it around with you.

I think we have to go a little bit further. If you're going to have self-replenishing prosperity, why not have self-replenishing love? Also self-replenishing happiness, joy, right friendship, and unlimited goodness. Add what you want to your *I am*. You'll get what you want to the exclusion of what you don't want, because the mind can only think one thought at a time. Say *I am a great father. I am a great husband.* If you're going to be in a mutually bonded relationship, why not make it great?

One of the rights of prosperity is that you've got the right to be fully loved. You've got a right not to be *alone*, but to enjoy the *all oneness* of the universe, which is only one L different from *alone*. Add one L and it becomes *all one*. We are all one, which means now that we are integrating for the first time on this planet, at higher, better, and more utopian levels. One of Bucky Fuller's great books is called *Utopia or Oblivion*. I think oblivion is untenable and unacceptable, and we have to create fundamental abundance to prevent it. With the breakthroughs in technology, for the first time in history, it is totally doable. We can create utopia now.

Walt Disney, who was a great example of prosperity, once called up his friend, entertainer Art Linkletter, and said, "Be ready at two'clock on Sunday afternoon. We're going for a little ride down to Orange County." They arrived in a city called Anaheim, and it was nothing but orange trees everywhere. Disney got him out of the car, started walking him around, and said, "Can't you see it, Art? There's Future Land. There's Cinderella's Castle. There's Pirates of the Caribbean." Disney could visualize the future Disneyland stretched out in front of him.

Because Art knew that Disney had repeatedly pushed the edge of his finances and crashed and burned, having blown away so many fortunes and so much wealth, with every step Art took, he was saying, "No, no, no, I will not invest in this dream of Walt's." He couldn't see what Walt was envisioning and creating. Disney may have gone down, but he was always looking up. As a futuristic, visionary artist and dreamer, he drew a picture of where he wanted to go fifty years in advance.

Disney envisioned a city of the future called EPCOT (Experimental Prototypical Community of Tomorrow). After his death in 1966, his company abandoned the idea of an actual city and instead created a theme park based on technological innovation called Epcot Center, which opened at Disney World in Orlando, Florida, in 1982. In 2019, the whole Disney World complex attracted 20.4 million visitors from around the world. It's the most visited theme park in the world.

Each of us should be deeply inspired to have fifty- and hundred-year goals, like Walt Disney. It is free to dream, to have great visions and a destiny worthy of you. You can leave a great and inspiring legacy as Walt did.

When you set goals, make them long-range and give them permanence. Leave something behind you. It doesn't matter what it costs.

When the late Dr. Robert Schuller Sr. was planning to build the magnificent Crystal Cathedral in Garden Grove, California, he was talking to its architect, Philip Johnson. Johnson asked, "How much money have you got?"

Schuller says, "I haven't got any."

"That won't do anything," said Johnson. See, if you think with your pocketbook, you think about what you *can't* do rather than what you *can* do.

Ultimately, Schuller struggled, strained, and built a magnificent, one of a kind church that people will visit for a thousand years.

Schuller said, "Make the decision, and then find the provision." It sounds like gobbledygook, but I promise you, that's the way it works. Walt Disney never said, "Oh, my God. What is this going to cost?" It doesn't matter. Infinite amounts of money are available to the likes of Disney and Schuller—and to you and me.

Infinite resources are available to you and me as well.

Right now, say aloud, *Infinite resources are available to me.*

Say, *I'm meeting all the people I need to meet right now.*

Why can I tell you that there is infinite wealth available to you? Because if you're made in the image and likeness of God, as it says in Genesis 1:26, then you are infinite. If God made the whole universe, then he is the causeless cause, the *a priori* intelligence in the universe, the intelligence before reason.

If God is dealing with infinity and you and I are made in God's infinite image, then you and I are dealing with infinity, which makes us infinite.

Right now, say aloud, *I'm infinite.*

How do you build self-esteem? You know the saying, "Love your neighbor as yourself." It means you're going to have to love you before you love anyone else, and more than anyone else loves you. Then the love will flow out of you like water off a duck's back.

Now touch yourself and say, *I like me.*

If you don't like you, no one else can. You have to tell yourself *I like me* fifty to a hundred times a day to build your own self-esteem.

To alter that slightly, say, *What good things are happening? What happy, prosperous things are happening to me?* How are you making your life and everybody else's better off and no one's worse off? How is that happening in your experience? When you ask and answer those questions, you'll upgrade your thinking. You can transform your life just with some positive self-talk and positively leading questions.

I teach individuals to build their self-esteem. As I said above, each of us has to positively and correctly like and love themselves. If you repeat, *I like me!* fifty plus times a day for at least a month, your self-esteem will skyrocket upward. You just expanded your thinking and self-image.

I once sat on an airplane with a lady who was struggling with what her parents called a sleazebag of a boyfriend. I asked her, "Well, is he?"

"I guess you'd have to say that he is."

After a fairly deep conversation, I said to her, "A couple of quick questions: if you're with him five years from now, are you going to be happy?"

"No way."

"Five years from now, you're carrying that man's baby. Are you going to be happy?"

"No way."

"Then why are you with him?"

"If I wasn't with him, I'd be lonely."

I convinced the lonely lady above to use this following affirmation, which all of us occasionally need to have in our memory repertoire.

Say now, *I like me when I'm alone.*

The trinity is: (1) *I like me.* (2) *I like me alone.* (3) *I like me with other people.* That covers our self-esteem thinking simply and memorably in 360 degrees of comprehensiveness.

Bucky said, "If you're going to do anything, be a comprehensive and anticipatory design scientist," meaning, look at the whole entire picture from the inside out. Anyone can do their own little finite thinking, but why not figure out how to make the whole picture bigger, brighter, more outstanding, and more outrageous for all of us? As your self-esteem goes up, that in turn encourages everybody else around you. Your good example will escalate their self-esteem. As everyone's self-esteem rises, you can more profitably predict the future.

When you're profitably predicting the future, it's an inside out game. You need to know where to look and what to look for, and where to look is inside. Christ said, "The kingdom of God is within you," so you've got to look inside.

Every morning at 7:30, Walt Disney said to his staff, "My imagination creates my reality." Imagination is the beginning of every manifestation, relation, and materialization. I imagined I would be doing my seminars when I was bankrupt, upside down, and didn't totally like myself or what was happening to me. I imagined I would be talking to people that care about things that matter, that would make a life-transformative difference. I create my own reality.

Say it in the first person: *I create my own reality.*

There was a movie by Francis Ford Coppola called *Peggy Sue Got Married.* Peggy Sue is unhappy with her life. She has a twenty-year time warp where she goes back in time. She talks to a nerd who basically says, "I want advice and what's going to cut it?" Peggy Sue tells him if he wants to cut it in the big time, he should invest in huge, gigantic, portable radios, miniature TVs, tennis shoes, and pantyhose. The movie came out in 1986, so this all made sense.

In 1967, there was *The Graduate,* featuring Dustin Hoffman. Hoffman, playing the title role, is told that the future is in plastics.

Another 1986 film, *Short Circuit,* foretold that artificial intelligence would be the way to go. In it, a robot equipped with artificial intelligence breaks into a lady's house, reads the *Encyclopedia Britannica* in a nanosecond, watches TV, and dances with her like John Travolta.

The point here with regard to prosperity is that art frequently predicts the future of business. Intuitive artists, movie makers, and writers can often accurately foresee where big money will be made. Ask your inner knower to correctly tell you what is going to happen, based on the movies that you watch, and thus where to profitably invest.

Now the question is, in the future, are there going to be more or fewer opportunities?

There will be more opportunities, with four billion entrepreneurial people—the second half of the world population coming online, thanks to cell phones, satellite communications, 5G, and so on.

I believe that attitude is just about everything. You have a bottom-line attitude whereby either you think you can or you think you can't. With a positive mental attitude, you can create an extraordinary future.

Tony Robbins became famous by popularizing walking on fire to break the chains of one's fears. He is a master of a mind control method called NLP (neurolinguistic programming) and teaches it worldwide. He's inspired millions of people to walk on fire and not get burned, and has published a best seller called *Unlimited Power.*

Tony taught me a tool of empowerment such that you can wake up and in thirty seconds feel like a 10 every morning. He said the most empowering word known to man or woman is *yes.*

Pretend it's the last thirty seconds of a game between your favorite sports team and its biggest rival. The game is tied. If you cheer loud enough, smashing your hands together and screaming yes!, they will win.

First thing tomorrow morning, stand in front of a full-length mirror in your bedroom naked, no matter who's looking on—spouse, partner, or kids. Inhale deeply and shout, *Yes, yes, yes!*

If you do that, you'll say, along with that Helen Reddy song, "I am invincible." You'll end up touring the whole world and traveling first class, which is what I recommend. Ultimately, you will end up in Paris, and you'll stay at the most luxurious of hotels, all of which have paper-thin walls. You will have fifteen hours of jet lag, you'll be ready to go on a bus tour at six in the morning, and you'll be shouting *yes!* in front of the mirror. The Parisians in the next room will say, "Those beautiful Americans!" (If you believe that, I've got an oceanfront property for you in Colorado.)

As Jim Rohn used to say, attitude determines your potential and beliefs. Your potential and beliefs determine the action you take, which determine the results you get.

Here's the point. Who owns your attitude? You do.

What am I asking you to do? Adopt a rich attitude on a conscious and subconscious basis so as to fix it into your thought, so as to make prosperity as one of your magnificent obsessions, not to the exclusion to the rest of life but to the inclusion. Prosperity is just one of the vehicles, one of the conveniences, that give you more options.

We're in the time of more options. When I grew up, TV had three channels. Today you've got over five hundred options. If you know where to find me on TV, I'm on twenty-four hours a day. It is amazing. You can get anything you want.

Jesus said that it's done unto us according to our beliefs (Matthew 9:49). You are as rich as you believe you can be. If you change your belief positively, you'll get richer. If you change your belief negatively, you'll get poorer. That's why the rich get richer: because they can have a rich mindset.

Your mindset creates your money set. You essentially have a thermostat in your mind that says, "I am worth this much," and that's how much you will earn or create. And you can change it, just like a thermostat. I am asking you to change the money-creating thermostat in your mind. Raise your money-creating thermostat, please, and make everyone better off.

Economically ignorant anti-business politicians, entitled children, and scholars say, "We ought to divide up the wealth and give away a universal income." They want to share everybody else's tax money. Everyone who has truly earned their own money will tell you that you can't share money that way, because if you take away all the money of the rich, they will get it back again by right of their own consciousness. Christ said, "For to the one who has, more will be given, and from the one who has not, even what he has will be taken away." (Mark 4:25).

Haveness is our state of consciousness. The rich are rich because of their state of consciousness. Each of us has to create our own rich state of consciousness to become and stay forever rich. The money keeps rolling in for individuals who have cultivated, curated, and mastered a rich state of consciousness.

Producer Merv Griffin created a new game show at a rate of one a month, and every one of them was a hit. Why? Because he essentially said to himself, "I know how to keep creating a new game show every month," and the ideas kept coming thundering into his awareness. In lay language he was saying: "My business is clicking."

On the other hand, my mother said to my brothers and me, "If you get cold feet, you will get a cold." I have reprogrammed myself to never again get a cold. However, I have a lot of warms.

To this day, when I fly in to cold areas, I bring galoshes, because of that thought form, emotively impressed by my mother. It imploded into my subconscious, so it explodes in my experience. I cannot eradicate it.

I go skiing with my wife, and I sweat with the best of them. I get icicles in my hair. She says, "Oh, my God. If you get a cold, wet head, you will get a cold."

I say, "My mother never told me that, so I don't and won't believe that."

Neither one of these beliefs has any basis in reality, but all of us have grown up with different thoughts implanted in us, and they implode unforgettably in our imagination. We have been told what we can and what we can't do and how rich we can and can't be, and that becomes a controlling factor in our experience.

Self-help author and businessman W. Clement Stone started with nothing as a salesman and went forward to build an insurance company, and with his Aon Corporation, he ended up a billionaire. He used to say, "If you have everything to gain and nothing to lose by trying, by all means try."

Why not find out how prosperous you can become? That may mean you have to originate a new deal deep within yourself. It may mean you have to be in alignment with your higher, spiritual self.

There are times when everyone is swept forward. Steve Jobs and Steve Wozniak were Master Mind partners when they started Apple. Every one of the fifty-eight people that were in and around at the time became a multimillionaire.

If you set your business or investments up right, they will be endlessly profitable and self-replenishing. Bucky Fuller taught me that money growth is unlimited. Why is it unlimited? Because I am unlimited. I am made in the image of an infinite creator; therefore I have infinite ability, skills, and talents to create infinitely. That's true of all of us.

There's enough money now that the eight billion alive now on earth could all be millionaires, because we have an infinite conceptual economy.

You might say, "It's not infinite in my experience." I'm going to show you where it's infinite. People can create and trade goods and services without limit. The only limit is in our thinking. The point is, if you change your perception, you change your result.

6

The Size of the Pie

When I came to California to start buying real estate, I found vastly appreciated prices for homes and rentals; it was scary to me. Mike Ferry, a superstar real estate agent and speaker, recommended that I invest in real estate with negative cash flow.

I said, "Negative cash flow? Why would I want that?"

He said, "We don't call it that here in California."

"What do you call it?"

"Extended down payment."

"Extended down payment! What a great idea."

Michael sold me an assumable loan for a home worth $80,000, and I sold it three years later for $358,000. Now that's serious appreciation. It taught me that when you change your perception, you change your results.

Once, back in the eighties, I was in Austin, Texas, on Kathy Cronkite's TV show. She's the daughter of legendary news anchor Walter Cronkite. She's a brilliant, elegant, gorgeous lady, but she was also into journalism that attacks and goes for the jugular.

I knew what she was going to talk about. At the time, Americans were offended by the large amount of real estate that the Japanese were buying up. It was all over the papers when I was down there, and I knew she was going to jump all over it. "The Japanese, it says on the headline of *USA Today*, bought $18 billion worth of real estate and Americans ought to shudder and worry," Kathy boomed.

Before I went on, a guy backstage said, "Watch it. You'd better be on your mental toes and ready to handle this."

I said, "I can handle it."

The guy in the control booth said, "Ms. Cronkite, thirty seconds to airtime."

I said, "Kathy, there's one thing I've got to tell you before we go on air."

"What's that?"

"My daddy loved watching your daddy on TV. When your daddy said, 'And that's the way it is,' my daddy was sure that that was the way it was, because your daddy came out of integrity."

"Ten seconds to airtime," said the guy in the control booth.

I went on, "I have to tell you that your daddy is the only guy in media that has not been hung upside down by his toenails in abject pain like the rest."

"Three seconds to airtime, two, one."

I could see her replete with emotion. Why? As Dale Carnegie said, "You attract more bees with honey than you do with vinegar." You've got to use good human relations all the time, even if you don't like the person. I like and respected Kathy and what she had to do to make the show interesting and provocative. However, I planned to look good and handle the media as a winner and thinker with messages that positively matter.

When she asked the question about foreign ownership of real estate, I smiled and said, "America is a land of immigrants. Great people, like my parents, who came from Denmark, were all foreign at one time. The only people that deserve to own this place are the Indians. Ask them if they believe in immigration. Indians believed in the common wealth, meaning the water, land, and animals were owned and to be used by everyone. In 1626, they sold Manhattan Island to Peter Minuit for $24 worth of beads and trinkets. The Indians that sold it didn't actually own it or even understand the negotiation. American history books record it as the greatest business trade ever."

I shared with you what I shared on TV because I want you to outthink any and all future interrogators.

Everybody is your customer, or you're their customer. That's the way the world works: we're all here to serve one another, and you want to serve the highest and best. I knew what Kathy had to do—she wanted to be an intriguing interviewer that delivered a biased point of view—but she didn't know what I could do.

I said that the Japanese participated aggressively in Black Monday—the big stock market crash of 1987—because they learned something by studying Nathan Rothschild. Nathan's father, Meyer Amschel Rothschild, started the first international bank in modern Europe. He got each of his five sons to open a bank simultaneously in five different countries. The market wanted an international bank so they could trade and do commerce more seamlessly. When the news was announced, all businesspeople decided to participate in his brilliant new creation, and commenced banking with Rothschild's international bank.

In 1815, the British and their allies were facing Napoleon at Waterloo, and the result of the battle would determine how the markets would go. Rothschild had the information six hours before everyone else. He started selling the market short, implying that he knew Napoleon had won the battle. Everybody else saw him and said, "This guy knows what he's doing. We'll sell the market short." Rothschild bought the whole market for half of a penny on a pound. When the news came that the British had won, he became a millionaire in one day.

I explained to Kathy, "The Japanese learned that would be a good technique. Today, because everything is done by computer debit, they decided in one day to take all their money back home and play with it. Our market crashed and burned. When the market went down, they came back in, bought in, and made a fortune. All of this was totally legitimate and legal.

"On the other hand, when the Japanese bought $18 billion worth of real estate, they were not taking it home. We want foreign nationals to actively buy and circulate their money in American real estate. They believed that our economy is very strong and this is the right place to put money. Know that the whole world economy, Kathy, is based on the U.S. dollar; it's the reserve currency and everyone in the world trades with it only.

"Kathy, what happened in real fact is that last year, just in the United States of America, we sold $6 trillion worth of real estate, so that $18 billion is less than the equivalent of a fingernail clipping of money. It is an irrelevant fact that media has hyped as something that we should be frightened about. In fact, what I want is more dollars, more goods, more trade, more transportation paid for by foreign nationals."

I traveled abroad and studied in multiple foreign countries. I learned their business practices, their languages, and their customs. I learn that people lived together by living together not by breathing animosity, hatred, hurt and pain, and disagreement. Fear stifles all of us, especially fear of somebody else.

As Cavett Robert said, "It's not how big a piece of the pie you get, my friend. It's how big you make the pie." The only place that the pie exists is in the same place we've been talking about—in the mind. The more good you've got, the more good you can give to other people. You can't give something if you haven't got it.

Say, *I've got it*, and then you'll get it. You'll make the whole world better off, because there's enough money for all of us to do it. Fred J. Young said, "Any normal, healthy American can make him or herself a millionaire if he or she wants to badly enough, starts it early enough, and works at it hard enough." My only disagreement is, what is early enough? *Early enough* is a relative term.

The story of Markita Andrews is so enchanting that I put it in the original *Chicken Soup for the Soul* book. She lived in Brooklyn, New York. When she was eight and a half, Markita's dad split the scene. Markita's mom knew the principles I'm teaching you: figure out what you want, and put it in writing. Put pictures of what you want on walls. Markita had pictures on her personal storyboard.

When she was fourteen, Markita wanted to travel around the world. Mrs. Andrews said hopefully, "Markita, you'll make enough money to take Mom and you around the world, won't you?" Great vision.

Markita joined the Girl Scouts. The Girls Scouts magazine said if you sell more Girl Scout cookies than anyone, you win a trip around the world, all expenses paid, for you and the whole family.

Kids intuitively know if you want to cut it, you've got to get a Master Mind partner. Her aunt was a great salesperson in real estate. Markita asked, "How do you sell?"

"Always wear your right outfit, your professional garb, your Girl Scout outfit," said her aunt. "When you're doing business, dress like you're doing business. Go up to people in the apartment buildings from 4:30 to 6:30 p.m., especially on Fridays. Ask for a big order. Always smile. Whether they buy or not, be nice to them, Markita. Don't ask them to buy your cookies; ask them to invest."

Markita would come up to someone and say, "I'm earning a round-the-world trip for Mom and me merchandising Girl Scout cookies. Would you like to invest in one dozen or two dozen?"

When you're persuading somebody, nod your head, smile, and be very polite and friendly, because if they don't buy today, they might come back and buy tomorrow.

Markita sold 42,000 boxes of Girl Scout cookies. She went on to have a best-selling book called *How to Sell More Cookies, Condos, Cadillacs, or Anything*. Disney did one of their top movies on her, called *The Cookie Kid*.

You may say, "You can only succeed if you're an extra-vert." I want to debunk that and similar theories. Whatever you assume is true probably causes you to have a money problem, and is probably not true. Success doesn't depend on having a college education—not that that is bad, but a college degree in itself doesn't mean that you'll make it.

At one point, I was being filmed at an event with Markita, and I met her backstage. She was tall, thin, and painfully shy. She would have been a wallflower if she'd had the opportunity. If you'd asked me if she could have pulled off what she had accomplished, I would have said, "Probably no way," from external criteria," but prosperity doesn't come from externals. It comes from internals and from your desire. If you've got a white-hot desire, a magnificent obsession, there's nothing that can hold you back. Markita had a burning desire and ambition to treat her mother and aunt to a trip around the world and became the best Girl Scout cookies salesperson ever at that time.

Motivational speaker Denis Waitley was on the same program. He observed, "Success is not reserved for the talented. It is not in the high IQ, not in the gifted birth. Not in the best equipment. Not even in ability. Success is almost totally dependent upon drive, focus, and persistence!"

As Robert Schuller's Possibility Creed would say, "If you're confronted with a mountain, you go over, under, around, or through. There's always a gold mine on the other side." If you have what New Yorkers call galloping chutzpah, or positive audacity, you will get whatever you truly want.

Anyhow, on this program Markita comes innocently out on stage in front of the meanest-looking man that I've ever seen. This guy looks like he'd eat his young. She's on live TV and says, "Mister, would you like to invest in one dozen or two dozen boxes of Girl Scout cookies?"

Angrily he said, "I don't buy any Girl Scout cookies. I am a federal penitentiary warden. I put two thousand rapists, robbers, criminals, muggers, thugs, and child abusers to bed every night."

Markita was solid. See, in every situation, somebody's selling and somebody's buying. There's a translation of consciousness, a transference of awareness. Either you are self-persuaded that you can do it, or somebody else can unpersuade you.

Markita smiled really big. She said, "Mister, if you take some of these cookies, maybe you won't be so mean and angry and evil."

I don't remember his next retort, but it was venomous. He was bad.

Markita, "Mister, not only that, but I think you'd be well advised to take some for every one of your two thousand prisoners."

I couldn't believe it. This guy pulled out a checkbook and wrote a check on the spot.

I wish I could tell you all the stories I've got in my head about people who were about to ask for an order. They go out to lunch. They have a few drinks. They think twice as big. They ask for, and get, twice the biggest order just because they asked for it.

I started saying, "I want to sell a million copies of my book *Dare*." My client at California Paramedical and Technical College immediately came up and said, "Here's a check. I want to buy the first five hundred, and I want you to sign one for every one of the graduating students." I wouldn't even have thought to do that. I promise you now, I think to do that.

The bottom line is, you're prosperous no matter what— whether somebody else does a deal with you, doesn't do a deal with you, does business with you, or doesn't do business with you. That does not affect your prosperity any more than you would let yourself be rejected unless you give yourself permission to be rejected.

Millionaires are not unusual. In fact, *Forbes* magazine reports we have more than one new billionaire in America daily. To become rich, wealthy, and prosperous, individuals work hard, smart, and differently. Most did what they loved. Their work became their play, and they did it with common things. Most people say, "They're celebrities or movie stars." Not true. These account for less than one tenth of 1 percent of Americans. The real wealth belongs to people that work ten or twelve hours a day; they've been doing it for years, and most of them are post forty-five. Usually they're still married to their first spouses, so if you're not married yet, you could still do it.

I read a magazine article that listed the most unusual kinds of millionaires, and the group that has the most millionaires, curiously, is dry cleaners. Why? Their business is always cleaning up.

The principle here is obvious, though. Most of the dry cleaners that I know are from a foreign country, and they had the perception that in America, the opportunity is great. Our dry cleaner happens to be from India, a husband and wife team. They also own several pizza businesses. They own their own Mercedes. They hire a lot of people, but they drive up every day to clean up the place. They work extraordinarily hard, and they're very quiet about their wealth.

Most people assume that medical doctors and lawyers are the ones with all the wealth. Not true. It's said that you're twice as likely to become a millionaire as a salesperson than as a lawyer or a doctor, which is of interest because sales jobs are relatively easy to obtain and are available in both good and bad economies. Sales is said to be the highest paid hard work and the lowest paid easy work in the world. I want to suggest to you the good news that you don't have to have capital. You've got to have the idea and be able to believe in it enough to be convincing.

The best way to generate money is with sales: sell your idea, product, service, or patent to someone.

If you can't sell, partner with somebody else who has great sales ability, power, and the connections. That's what Master Minding is about: the two of you together form a third new, invisible mind in an alliance that can do what you can't do individually.

My friend and client Peter J. Daniels was totally illiterate until he was twenty-six. Somebody read him a copy of *Think and Grow Rich.* Peter started to study success for seven hours a day. Now he is one of the richest men in the world and has headquarters in Adelaide and Singapore. The street corners he used to fight on, he now owns.

In fourth grade, he had a teacher named Mrs. Philips, who used to rattle his chain and say, "Peter J. Daniels, you're no good. You're a bad apple. You're never going to amount to anything."

Peter wrote a new book called *Mrs. Philips, You Were Wrong.* Every one of us has had a Mrs. Philips in our life. They could be a parent, a spouse, a kid, an employer, an associate, a person that considers himself your friend. They put you down so they don't feel as bad about themselves, because if you really cut the mustard and they are into comparison, they will feel bad. He and I do tons of work together. He taught me that if you draw a dot in Singapore and draw an arc three thousand miles around it, you've got half the world's human population: about four billion people. Peter and I once were once talking, and he said, "Do you know what makes sure that you're not greedy? The one thing that makes sure that you're not greedy is if you have it in your head and heart to be a giver."

Now my recommendation to you will be the same as Peter Daniels' was. Read biographies, autobiographies, and articles about success. Find out who the who's who in the world are, and then decide, "I'm part of the A party list." Write into your diary the names of everyone you want to and plan to meet. You will be surprised at how it happens.

Let's discuss your potential. Your potential is infinite. I am suggesting there is infinitely more in you than you imagine, have thought about, or tried to use. Let's look at what the Bible says and secondly, at a very popular book that has inspired readers to believe in their human potential through the eyes of a seagull who challenges his fullest talents, skills, and abilities. The Bible says in Deuteronomy 1:11: "May the LORD, the God of your fathers, make you a thousand times as many as you are and bless you, as he has promised you!" God wants to promote you, encourage you, excite you, show you favor, bless you, and increase you a thousand times more.

We get stuck in our finite thinking and forget that with God, all things are possible. He wants to multiply you a thousand times; that's his promise. When I was in high school in the sixties, my father earned maybe $5,000 a year working eighteen hours a day in his bakery.

Inspired by the vast success of the Beatles, I started a rock band called the Messengers. Once my band was rocking, I could rent venues and get two thousand high school rockers to pay five dollars each to come out to a dance. I was making over $5,000 in one night, an amount of money that took my father a year to earn.

That is what I want you to consider in your life: you have infinitely more unexplored potential. God desires to bless you a thousand times more. Don't talk yourself out of it, saying, "I don't really deserve all that." Yes, you do. You and I are children of the Most High God. I want you to express and experience a thousand times more wisdom, joy, happiness, love, success, prosperity, and all of life's fulfillments. You have to decide to use your God-given potential and the full spirit being within, and you will come alive and thrive. Prosperity will gush towards you.

Many of us learned this truth about our untapped potential in Richard Bach's best-selling book *Jonathan Livingston Seagull.* In that book we learned there's only one person to compare yourself with, and that's you.

Only compare your potential with yourself. Decide where you are and how far you think you can go in every area of your life. Your potential is vastly more than you currently think it is. Only you can test it, and test it some more. There's no one for you to compare with: you are unique. You are one of a kind: there's never been anyone like you before, nor will there ever be again. You're here at the university of earth to maximize your potential. You were meant to metaphorically be Jonathan Livingston Seagull, an unstoppable high-flying, seagull that loves life and living full out. You are here to catch the message and teach it, because many people are disadvantaged, with inaccurate information about their personal potential. We all have ten times more potential than we use.

7

The Art of Hugging

My wife and I did a national hug survey once. We discovered that 83 percent of us grow up in families that got less than one hug a day, and 98 percent of us want more hugs than we've been getting. The Self-Esteem Institute says you need four hugs a day to be normal, eight for maintenance, and twelve for growth. Once I was in Calgary, Canada, talking to an audience of five hundred, mostly men. I said, "If you guys aren't stuck in your machoism, I'd love to hug all of you."

When you're hugging someone shorter than you—I'm six feet four and hug a lot of people every year—bend your knees. Short people don't want whiplash. When you're with little kids, get down to their eye level and hug. With his Center for Attitudinal Healing, Dr. Jerry Jampolsky, author of *Love Is Letting Go of Fear*, taught us that all kids need more hugs and that little boys get fewer kisses and hugs than little girls, because we think hugging is OK for little girls. If you've got little boys in your life, they deserve hugs and kisses too.

Also, when you're in a hug, be in a hug. So many people hug teepee to teepee—ever see that?—or they give you the old right hip, and they give you the old left hip. The guy that's not sure of his masculinity tries to burp you, break you, or bend you.

When you're in the hug, be in the hug. On the way out of a hug, make sure you reestablish good eye contact. Lock into the person's eyes, and if your self-esteem is such that you can handle it, inwardly verbalize and cast the enchantment, "I love you." You don't have to say it out loud. They'll get it telepathically.

Many people are handicapped, culturally deprived, or physically challenged, and we're here to serve them as resources. You can only do it if you've got it. The day you don't feel good about yourself, go into a convalescent home and hug someone who's had a stroke and is now aphasic, meaning that he can't articulate his words; he has half a mind in a human body. Hug him, and he'll take your hand and kiss it, and tears will form in his eyes. It'll reintegrate you to remember that you're a human being and that you are here to give love and serve greatly.

If you want to know whether greed is too much of a factor in your life, make sure that you keep giving. Make sure your charitable tendencies are such that you give while you're living and when you're gone, you give even something more. Leave something with permanence, like Andrew Carnegie, who created libraries around the world, or Dr. Norman Vincent Peale, who created the Horatio Alger Awards for Distinguished Americans. It's an award of which I am a proud recipient: each winner has come from rags to riches and been excessively philanthropic. We have raised enough money to give scholarships to tens of thousands of deserving at-risk kids, who graduate college with one of us as a mentor and proceed to do amazing wonders. See their website: Horatioalger .org. Whatever you give, plan now to give something that is bigger and more lasting than you.

The Dead Sea is only dead because it takes and doesn't give. It's a wasteland of hypersalinity, because it only takes in water; nothing flows through and out. You and I aren't meant to go through life being constipated. I do a little talk now at Sunday church services around the world called "You Sow It, and God Will Grow It."

Life gives to givers and takes from takers. One of the places where you've got to sow it is in your giving nature. I want you to give financially. I want you to give your energy. I want you to give your time. I want you to give your effort. I want you to give your smiles. I want you to give magnetic eye contact. I want you to give at levels at which you've never previously decided to give. I also want you, in your own heart of hearts, to pledge what you're going to give in the future to the spiritual source that serves you, nourishes you, edifies you, and helps you to become all that you can be. People will say, "I always give a buck at church," but if you snooze, you lose, going through life. Find out how much you believe in these laws and principles. People who give the most live the most wonderful, fulfilling, and joy-filled lives.

Giving is living; caring is sharing. The question is, how much are you giving? Once I got to speak at the biggest sheriff's department in the world, the Los Angeles County Sheriff's Department. All of the people in the audience—ten thousand of them—worked as volunteers. I couldn't believe it. We're talking about doctors, lawyers, bankers, businesspeople, housewives. They decided that they wanted to put on a police uniform and ride a horse or do search and rescue or go on patrol. Each of them had to go through 357 hours of academy work before getting to volunteer, giving up thirty-five hours a month.

I spent time with them at lunch. I got to spend the entire day with them. I hugged a good part of them. Those people were living at the leading edge of life because they decided to give at levels I've never seen before. They were only reimbursed $1 a year by the sheriff's department, and that's only for one reason: in case they got blown away in the line of duty, they're compensated with insurance, or if they get hurt, they get their medical bills paid.

During World War II, the principle was that you never blew up churches. Everybody in every armament division in the whole world knew that. Inadvertently, American troops blew up a church in Northern Italy. The war was over; we'd signed the peace pact. Because there were only so many boats and airplanes available for travel, the soldiers didn't get to go home for another three months.

The American troops went to the citizenry and said, "Look, we really want to contribute. We really want to source you. We really want to serve you. There's no war. Let's get together. We would like to help you rebuild this church brick by brick. We would like to do that as our gift back to you." As I said earlier, America is the greatest country in the world because we're the givingest country in the world. If we ever see somebody that is hurting, we help them.

The troops and the villagers rebuilt the whole church. In front of this church, there was a seven-foot, six-inch crystal statue of Jesus Christ carved out of Carrara marble, the best marble that exists. They put the whole statue back together. They glued it; they fine-tuned it. They made it almost as elegant as it was originally, but the one thing that had been blown to smithereens in the bombing was Christ's hands.

The citizenry and the soldiers met and asked, "Should we get a set of false hands for this Christ statue, or should we put a marble plaque in front?" They chose to put a marble plaque in front, and it says, "Christ's only hands are yours. Christ's only eyes to see are yours. Christ's only heartbeat is yours."

While we're only here a short time and only one heartbeat away from eternity, I would hope that you would be a giver at bigger and better levels, because it will open up depths of prosperity you didn't even know you had available to you.

8

Your Prosperity Recognizes You

The biographical film *Gandhi* won the Oscar for Best Picture in 1982. Its producer, Richard Attenborough, was ready to make the film twenty years earlier. Why couldn't he do it? Because Ben Kingsley was only eight years old at the time. The movie wouldn't be the phenomenal classic it is if anyone other than Ben Kingsley had played Mahatma Gandhi.

The point is that God's delays aren't God's denials. You and I need to go forth in our life and be all that we can be, but we can't always know how.

If people are not on the path, then, unfortunately, a lot of them commit suicide. When they do, they watch their body fall and say, "Oh, no. I'm still here," because there's nowhere to go. Your spirit is eternal and lives forever.

The Netflix movie *Surviving Death* described interviews with over twenty thousand people who have died and miraculously returned to life. Every one of them said that when they went to the other side, they were told: "You are not done yet: you have more to do on earth."

It says in the Bible, "I am the Alpha and the Omega" (Revelation 1:8). Isn't that right? You are always here. You don't have anywhere to go. You're permanently living in eternity. This is not a dress rehearsal. Now the goal is to make it as good as you can make it. The question is how good can you make it?

There's a joke about a man in Florida whose wife dies and who receives a large amount of insurance money. He decides, "I'll have one last great fling before I go up into the blue ethers."

He gets his hair slicked back in black, goes to the cosmetologist, and gets silicone shots put in both cheeks so they're nice, rosy, and red. He goes down to the Ferrari dealership and gets a racing red Ferrari convertible. He goes out to the haberdashery and gets himself some good glad rags.

This guy is cruising through Florida, enjoying himself. All of a sudden, clouds form overhead. A bolt of lightning incinerates our friend Sam, and teleports him face-to-face with God. He says, "But, God, this is your boy, Sammy. Why me?"

God says, "Sammy, I didn't recognize you."

Your prosperity recognizes you. If you keep claiming it and aiming for it, you'll obtain it.

You probably know Émile Coué's famous and oft-heard affirmation: "Every day, in every way, I am getting better and better." What does that mean? I suggest to you that it takes a little extra, but the extra is all in the front end: you've got to put it in at the beginning. In marketing, they say, to do well, to be a smart marketer, find out what people want, need, and will pay for, and then give them more. Find out what they *don't* want, and give them less.

There was a gas station owner in Phoenix. His was just one of four gas stations on each corner. He started asking people, "If you could have anything you want at this filling station, what would it be?" They all said the same thing you and I would say: "Clean restrooms." He said, "That's it."

Remember, to make yourself magnificently and majestically prosperous, all you need is one idea, and then you've got to execute that one idea with superb and flawless excellence. It's more important to demonstrate than to teach prosperity.

This gas station owner triples the size of the restrooms, makes sure they are elegantly clean and are cleaned every twenty minutes. He puts original artwork on the wall. He puts in plush carpeting. He puts in an oversized throne. He puts on a $3,000 hand-carved door that says

"Gentlemen," and another $3,000 hand-carved door that says, "Ladies." On the way in, the employees give you a hot towel. On the way out, they give you a hot towel, and there's a red carpet going in and out.

In the men's room at the Madonna Inn in San Luis Obispo, California, there's a thunderous roar of water and pink lights come on when you step up to the urinal. It is heavenly, it is different, it is unusual, it is unforget-table. And you tell others about it, just as I am telling you. Remember, I said you have to work hard, smart, and differently. These two examples are clearly different, yet different in a better way.

If you find your unique factor and you start writing down your goals, you will achieve them. It's what Clem Stone said. His purpose statement was to make the world better for this and future generations.

I've already mentioned W. Clement Stone. At six-teen, he started selling because his mother owned a lit-tle insurance agency in a big insurance company. By age twenty, he decided to buy the insurance company that he was selling for. Now Clem was short in physical height and always had a pencil moustache.

W. Clement Stone, at age twenty, went in, smoking a stogie, and said, "I'm going to buy your insurance com-pany."

"What are you going to use for money?" asked the owner.

Clem smiled and said, "Yours." He was so bold, so brash, so bodacious that they gave it to him.

That's what is called a nothing-down deal. My writing partner on the book *The One Minute Millionaire,* Robert G. Allen, wrote *Nothing Down.* Bob sold twenty million copies, because everyone can afford to do nothing-down deals but rarely think they are possible or lack the courage to do them.

Study, think, and master the concept of nothing-down. You will start to master that business art form and become vastly profitable.

Today everybody's doing leveraged buyouts: LBOs. They're buying companies with the corporate's own assets, or at least not with their own money. If you can use somebody else's money, use it.

The effect is never greater than the cause. The creator is greater than his or her creation. Michelangelo was a greater painter, artist, and sculptor later in life than he was in the beginning. Who is the creator of your life?

Right now, touch yourself and say, *I am the creator of my life.*

Most of us don't understand that principle, however, and we become hung up in our hang-ups, so we become prisoners of our effects. My father, who went through the Depression, said to my brothers and me, "If you guys went through the Depression, like I did, you'd respect a buck. Who do you think I am, Rockefeller? Do you think money grows on trees? You're going to nickel and dime me to death."

When I was growing up, we lived by Naval Station Great Lakes in North Chicago, so he said, "You spend money like a drunken sailor. And you'd better save your money for a rainy day."

Most of us have heard those clichés and assume they are true. They are not. If you believe them and act on them, they will keep you poor and in poverty. It says in Joel 3:10, "Let the weak say, I am strong." We can translate to "Let the poor say, I am rich."

If I kept my father's point of view on prosperity, I would have a money rejection consciousness. He was good at hiding money in his shoe, in his belt, wherever you could hide money, because back then, you did not trust the bank. As far as he was concerned, the only thing you could trust was Hip Pocket National Bank.

You may say, "Christ was a poor carpenter." I want to apprise you that Christ was not poor. His father, Joseph, was traveling, which was rare in those times, had coin of the realm to stay in places, and was going to pay his taxes—meaning Joseph had earned money. Not only was Christ born into a family that had some substance, but he was a Jewish child that had three Arab kings bring him gold, frankincense, and myrrh—the extrabiblical report says that they came with camels of gold. Who knows for sure? The recorded stories are speculative, but it seems like a good launch into life, and totally deserved. Did you get that much when you were launched?

Jesus was said to wear seamless garments and that his clothes were radiant. I think that means that he, as a realized being, had a shining aura that he suggested could be duplicated: "Whoever believes in me will do the works I have been doing, and they will do even greater things" (John 14:12). If he were here today, he would be wearing Brioni clothes.

One day, Jesus had a little picnic. Five thousand people showed up. The Bible says he was preaching and teaching and went a little bit long. The disciples came up and said, "If you're so clairvoyant, clairaudient and clairsentient"— that means clear seeing, hearing, and feeling—"why did you plan this and forget to bring the food and the water?" They said, "We don't think it's a good day to be a disciple. We're going to ease out of here quietly, and hopefully nobody will recognize that we're associated with you."

Jesus said, "Bring me what you've got."

"This kid's got a little fish and bread. You aren't going to be feeding five thousand men with that" (not including the women and children). "We're leaving."

What did Jesus do? He took the little and turned it into abundance. Jesus fed five thousand plus people and had twelve baskets left over.

Jesus was thankful in advance. That's critical. It doesn't matter what you haven't got; it matters that you're looking forward to it. The more you get prosperity fixed in your thoughts and realize that more than enough is available, the faster you bring prosperity into a relationship with yourself.

Talk about surplus. Jesus took shortage and turned it into surplus with the one thing that's everything—the idea, the concept, and the knowingness.

You too can take lack, and with the right idea, turn it into lots, loads, abundance, and plenty. It doesn't matter what you haven't got or haven't been or haven't said or haven't thought. It matters where you're going. What's your destination?

There was a Vietnam war veteran who had his legs blown off. He went all the way across the country in two years and eight months, walking on his hands. He said he didn't care how long it took; it matters only that you know the direction that you're going in.

Right now, say, *I am really rich.*

Why? Because it exists—at levels that you didn't even know about. After twenty-five years of research, David McClellan at Harvard concluded that only 15 percent of success comes from product knowledge; 85 percent comes from good human relations skills and self-esteem. Yet most companies spend 85 percent of their time teaching product knowledge and technical skills. We're spending our time and money in the wrong place. The mental province is the one thing that creates everything out of nothing, and it always starts in the same place: as an idea in someone's mind.

You and I differ from all the other species on the planet in having the opportunity—as a matter of fact, the obligation—to do great, grand, and terrific thinking and take ourselves to absolutely new places that have never been gone to before.

I've already mentioned the late Robert Schuller Sr., who built the Crystal Cathedral. Here's a man who created a monument and who will have a lasting memory. He was a great theologian but also a phenomenal marketing genius, one of the greatest promoters I have ever had the privilege to experience.

At one point, Dr. Schuller and I were down in Boca Raton doing an international chiropractic meeting. I spoke first; Dr. Schuller was on second. Afterward we went to lunch together with all the doctors who earned over $1 million a year, all fifty-seven of them.

Dr. Schuller had just written a new book called *The Theology of Self-Esteem.* He said, "I want to make sure this gets to all three hundred thousand churches, temples, synagogues, ministers, priests, and rabbis around the country, and I want you to help." He pulled out a Cross ink pen and said, "This pen says *Robert Schuller* on it. I'd like somebody to start the bidding."

I went, "My goodness gracious," because this guy just got paid $10,000 to do a talk, and now he was raising more bread. The principle here—which is critical—is, if you are a believer and you know that you are serving the greater good, then you've got to be a great self-promoter. When you are a true believer, you grow into becoming a master at self-promotion. You've got to be willing to promote even when it infringes on your selfhood. If you know that that's the only way you're going to move forward, the way to move forward is to ask.

Anyhow, I was part of the bidding up to $200, at which time my wife kicked me under the table and said, "You don't even need a Cross pen. You've got hundreds of them at home." One guy gave him a check for $5,700 for that Cross pen. Before Schuller walked out of that luncheon, he had raised $78,000.

I suggest that Dr. Schuller is no different from you. It was uncomfortable for him to ask, but I witnessed him being a master asker, because he wanted to serve greatly and said he needed the financial support. God doesn't make any mistakes, so he put Dr. Schuller with high-earning doctors, and he asked for and got the support he requested.

When I lived in New York, Dr. Schuller came and charged thousands to attend his speech at Avery Fisher Hall, Lincoln Center. Schuller wanted to have an amazing rare organ from Avery Fisher Hall for his Crystal Cathedral church. He had all of us contributors stand up, and he said, "By the way, this thing costs $300,000, and you can buy one of its pipes for $1,000."

Dr. Schuller spoke for twenty minutes, and he came back and said, "Good. Thank you very much. We raised $380,000, and I bought the organ on the spot. God loves you, and so do I." I thought, "Whoa. This guy's cooking." It was an inspiration to me. When Dr. Schuller was building the Crystal Cathedral Church, he came up with a new methodology. As you know, when you have a problem, the first thing you do is write it down.

Second, you write down solutions—but he recommended ten outrageous solutions. One of them was: Find one guy to give me $6 million. John Crean, who owned Fleetwood International, which makes recreational vehicles, gave him $28 million.

The day that John and Donna Crean gave that money to Dr. Schuller, I watched them do it on TV. I immediately bought stock in Fleetwood International. I predicted what would happen after such an enormous tithe. Next day, Fleetwood stock tripled in price. The day after that, I sold it. Why? The principle is that anyone who gives is going to receive, and it comes in an overflowing, ever flowing abundance. It is good to make a profit and take your winnings off the table. The Old Testament gives you a tenfold return. Mark 10:29–30 gives you a potential of a hundredfold return. If you believe the story of the loaves and fishes, five thousand. *It is done unto you according to your belief.*

Then, Schuller said, "Find six people to each give me a million dollars." Crazy. Here's a guy with a thousand peo-

ple attending his church, and he's asking for these bodacious amounts live and on TV. Well, Bob Hope came up
and gave a million. John Wayne gave a million. Dr. Schuller
proceeded to get a million from Rich DeVos, cofounder of
Amway Corporation. W. Clem Stone, who was on Schuller's board of directors, said, "When you get the other five
million-dollar gifts, I'll give you a million."

Schuller's key quote is: "Nobody has a money problem,
only an idea problem." You want to memorize that idea,
repeat it to yourself four times a day for at least a month,
and take visceral ownership of it.

Many of us feel we aren't ready and aren't sure that we
deserve it or even desire it. *Think and Grow Rich* advises
to start going towards your prosperity at once, whether
you're ready or not.

9

Health, Family, and Friends

When you're writing what you want in your future diary, you ought to include good health goals.

I use a lot of humor in my work because it is one of the greatest facilitators of health in the world. The late Dr. Norman Cousins, author of *Anatomy of an Illness*, was diagnosed with a disease and given one in five thousand chances of living. The doctors said, "You're a goner."

Dr. Cousins had studied the effect of humor. He discovered that you could laugh your way out of disease. Laughter gets the endorphin system working and stimulates your body's entire immune system. When Cousins was sick and dying, he got every comedy film available and watched them continuously all day long. He cured himself of an incurable disease and lived to write, teach, and inspire the medical community to use humor on behalf of their patients. He discovered that there are thirty-four simultaneously interoperative chemistries in the mind, all of which are simultaneously operative when one button is pushed: having a sense of humor, whereby you laugh at yourself.

Cousins talked to cancer patients and taught them to figure out what they wanted, to have a selfless purpose that was bigger than they were, and to laugh uproariously at themselves once every day. He spoke to patients who had been told they would be dead in the next 30 days. He said, "The danger with this idea is that is if they buy into it, it becomes teleological: they go 29, 28, 27, 26, down to 1."

Cousins told the patients, "If you want to live, you've got to praise yourself, raise yourself, encourage each other, cheer each other and yourself on, and have a good sense of humor. Laugh every day. Find joy at every expression of your life."

The patients said, "Dr. Cousins, we've been telling you what's going right in our life. Our blood serology says we're all getting healthier and happier, and we're getting rid of all cancer."

Remember, you started with one cell. The zygote—the egg and the sperm—got together, so you're already a winner. The odds of you being here are 250 million to 1 against, so you're a winner. That one cell has been multiplying into prosperity for a long time, and if you stay happy, your body stays healthy. It's that simple.

That's why I teach with a heavy incidence of humor. I continually share jokes and humor with my family, staff, friends, audiences, and readers, because I want you to be happy, healthy, wealthy, and wise.

All of us are going to have problems. You are alive at the level of your problems. My late friend Dr. Norman Vincent Peale, author of *The Power of Positive Thinking*, used to tell me that every problem has a gift inside. You've got to unwrap the problem and find out what the benefit is. Dr. Peale would say that every adversity has a seed of an equivalent or greater benefit hidden inside it. It'll make you wonderfully well off if you look for the benefit.

The Mandinka Indians in Africa understand this. They take a problem, and once they all agree to what it is, they dance it, they sing it, and they have all the spirits come into them so they live into the solution of the problem. Hence they don't have any problems.

You and I have lots of health problems. Cavett Robert said, "If you've got any health problems, don't tell anybody about them, except your physician, and only if he or she asks." Cavett said the trouble with telling your friends about your health problems is that 80 percent of them don't care, and the other 20 percent are actually glad yours are worse than theirs.

This book is a comprehensive overview of true prosperity. If you're going to be truly prosperous, you've got to be healthy, and you've got to have good family goals. Have a replete family life, and write that into your complete goal list. If family has any meaning to you, as it does for me, write it in. Why not make your family life as exquisite as any other part of your life? Why not be a fully public, functioning human being? Why not see how good it can be when you get home, because you are also putting 100 percent into your family relationships?

That includes everybody in your household. In Southern California, many of us get Hispanic housekeepers. We've gotten one to live with us. She is magnificent. She smuggled herself out of Mexico, because America is a land of opportunity. She watched her twin sister fall headfirst into the rocks four hundred feet below and smash herself to smithereens.

What was she going to do? Go back to the Mexican government and say, "Look, my friend died. We were trying to escape. We're trying to emigrate, and we didn't make it"? Go to the Americans and say, "Would you come across the borderline and clean up my sister"?

We've helped Eva Espinoza become nationalized, which is a very interesting process: they go through many fiery hoops to accomplish this feat. When we arrived at the government building in Santa Ana, California, at six in the morning, there were already over five hundred people in line, waiting to pay to get to go through this process. We're in exciting times: people want to be here, and they'd like to be here legally and honestly.

Eva is part of our family. We've had many of our friends come over to our home. Many are shocked and ask, "Why would you let a housekeeper sit with you at dinner?" I say, "She's more family than you. If you keep this up, you don't get to stay or ever be invited back."

In the days of kings and queens, servers wore white gloves. They served, looked down (never at the boss), and then left the table. In more conscious situations, everyone is considered important, and housekeepers can sometimes eat with the family, except during parties or special festive occasions. It is a divine process. My children have grown up being bilingual in English and Spanish thanks to Eva.

In fact, I think in the future we owe it to ourselves and children to be multilingual. It is a minimum requirement. We've been very pretentious in America to think that everybody should learn how to speak English, when we don't even try to learn a second language.

I mean, as we start traveling around the world, most people in most foreign countries are multilingual. They're going to be more so. You go to India or China, and each of those countries have hundreds and hundreds of languages. In India, they speak Telugu, Kannada, Hindi, Urdu, and more. They all watch TV; they all learn English. It behooves us to let our kids learn other languages, especially before the age of twelve, when language is easier to learn. Why not have every child grow up multilingual?

If they learn one, then learning the second, third, and fourth are a piece of cake.

Let's move on to social life. My little book *Future Diary* recommends writing a list of two hundred people that you want to spend time with, play with, grow with, and be expanded by. You can write down anyone.

Let me illustrate this with a story. My wife and I had been traveling to Hawaii—vacationing there—for eight years. We were in a rental vacation resort hotel one holiday season with our great friend Dr. Peggy Bassette, whose non-denominational church of 17,000 people is headquartered in Huntington Beach, California—where I spoke quarterly and where we were married. Peggy came running back in from exercising and said, "You're not going to believe it. I just found a condo on Ali Drive, in Kona, for $25,000." That is the warm and dry side of the Big Island of Hawaii, which is our favorite place. We decided to go halves with Peggy, and rushed back with checkbooks in hand. We each put $125 down each and $100 a month, and seven years out, we ended up owning it. It's just exquisite.

Why did this happen? Because we all had it in our consciousness that we ought to have a starter place in Hawaii and advance from there. I really needed a place like that to cool out, because you need to balance out workaholism.

Burnout comes out of a lack of balance. Ecclesiastes says, "For everything there is a season" (Ecclesiastes 3:1), both work and rest. You're going to cool out: set the time that you're going to have as downtime, sabbatical time. You need to set it up in advance of work, so that you schedule rest, relaxation, and soul rejuvenation. Set Sabbath time in advance of starting the project. In fact, I would set a goal for you of three months' vacation a year.

To go back to my Hawaii story: we were over in Hawaii, and I was standing in the car rental line. The man next to me sneezed, and I said, "Gesundheit." He turned around, put out the hand he'd sneezed in, and said, "Hi, Mark. I've been in several of your seminars; delighted to see you here on the Big Island. I am head of economic development here in Hawaii, Mark." His name was Glen Taylor.

I shook his hand and said, "Chris Hemmeter's opening his Disneylike Hyatt here soon, isn't he?" This was back in the eighties.

If some of you don't know who the late Chris Hemmeter was, let me put him in context. Hemmeter didn't even have a high school education. He worked as a bellman and decided that he wanted to own the finest hotels— not just hotels, but destination resort hotels around the world, with him as their superstar developer. Now, that's a big, hairy, audacious goal.

Chris had already built and gained renown for the Hyatt Oahu. He did exceedingly well with it and built the most profitable hotel in the world: the Hyatt Maui.

Chris was also one of the best networkers in the world. When Jimmy Carter was president, Chris invited him to stay at his house in Oahu, which is really exquisite, I'm told. The next thing you know, he got to build the Jimmy Carter Library for $25 million.

On another occasion, Ronald Reagan was president, and Yasuhiro Nakasone was prime minister of Japan. Chris had both of them to stay at his house in Hawaii for their summit meeting. The next day he sold the Hyatt Maui to the Japanese.

What's the principle? You can network with anyone, but you must write down a hit list of two hundred people in advance. If you only know two or three, start there, and then keep adding. When you meet them, don't cross them out, like milk, eggs, and butter on a shopping list. In lavender, the high spiritual color of victory, write down, *Victory.*

In any event, I said to Glen, "I want to meet Hemmeter."

"Mark," he said, "the good news is that on September 2, we open up the Hyatt Waikoloa, which is on the north shore of the Kona Coast, and it will be the ultimate resort in the world. It has everything. When you arrive, you go through a laser holography show that is totally Disneyesque. You go by $3.5 million of Asian American artwork. You get into a gondola, or you take a monorail, and you go through the whole property to see it all before you arrive. They've got nineteen restaurants, all original. I've got two tickets. My wife doesn't want to go."

"My dear friend," I said, "is that an invitation?"

"If you want it to be an invitation, it's an invitation."

"Can I bring my wife?"

"I don't think I can wangle that."

I got to go when they dropped a quarter million orchids on us during the Hawaiian high kahuna's blessing of that place, with who's who from around the world. Why? I decided that I'm always in my right place.

Say out loud, *I'm always in my right place. Whatever is happening is happening wherever I am.*

You know the cliché: the ladder is only crowded at the bottom, never at the top. I believe that once you're prosperous, once your mind starts opening up, you'll bring a lot of other people up with you. As soon as you get closer to the horizon, you see a new horizon. Turn on your dream machine. Then don't let anyone turn it off. Build empires in your mind, empires that, like Walt Disney's, get built, maybe posthumously. It doesn't matter, because the excitement is in the actualization. Getting there is all the fun.

10

Green and Growing

With regard to finances, the brilliant and oft-heard cliché is: "If your go-out exceeds your income, then your upkeep will be your downfall." Your earning power has to always be greater than your spending power.

There are two aspects here. One is earning power; the other is net worth. You must have in writing what you want your earning power to be; write it down by the day, the month, and the year. Keep making it bigger and bolder than it was the month before. If you cease to grow, financially speaking, you begin to die. You begin to doubt your moneymaking abilities and prowess.

I've got friends in the speaking business who earn $6 million a year and spend $7 million a year. Not good, baby. What you get to keep is called your net earnings, and that's all that matters. Too many people overspend and live on their gross income, ignorantly thinking it is their net income. You can have a little business, be more profitable, and live better than somebody who owns a big business but doesn't know how to be profitable. Keep it small, and keep it all.

Make sure that you're green and growing, because when you are ripe, you're rotten, and when you're blue, you're through. Make sure that you are always slightly outside your comfort zone, because you only grow when you're outside your comfort zone, when you are stretched to achieve more than you have before. That's what makes life exciting and thrilling.

Write down in detail the requisite actions that you're going to take. They asked billionaire H. L. Hunt, "What does it take to be rich?" He said exactly what I've told you: Number one, you've got to know what you want. Number two, what will you sacrifice to get it?

You don't have to make any ridiculous sacrifices. You certainly don't have to sacrifice your family, unless that's what you want. One of my closest friends, who makes $24,000 a day, got divorced from his third wife because he's so enamored of business. He sacrificed his love life and his wife for more money. It's a painful and time-consuming problem, which, with more thoughtful balance and written goals, could have been avoided.

Walt Disney taught me that when your values are clear, decision making is easy. I'm saying that you can have it all.

In the movie *Auntie Mame*, Auntie Mame says, "Life's a banquet, but most poor suckers are starving to death," not because they have to starve, at least not in America. If anyone's hungry in America, it's not because we don't have Salvation Armys, Goodwills, thrift stores, and multiple charitable organizations ready, willing, and wanting to serve the needy; it's because the hungry don't know where to go for help. I have spoken to many of these fine organizations and know that they will take good and abundant care of those in need of food, clothing, shelter, training, and jobs—all for free.

I've met people who say, "I just don't want to go where they're feeding the poor, ignorant, and indigent." I reply, "What? You're down and out, and someone is trying to help you, and you refuse their loving assistance?" As Zig Ziglar used to say, "You can't help someone who doesn't want any help."

In any event, write down your goals over the short term, middle term, and long term, at least five years in advance. On an annual basis, jot down how much money you're going to give yourself, five years in advance.

Calvin Hunt is in the life insurance business. He wrote down that he wanted to earn a quarter million dollars at age thirty-three—not per year, but per month. He called me up and said, "I can't believe it. I just sold a $15 million whole life policy. I earned $385,000 on one sale."

How do you explain it? I said, "You knew what you wanted, you wrote it down, you lived up to your full potential, and you kept listening and being inspired by my audios."

Your belief system has to stay pumped up, because all of us either are pumped up or let the world mind erase our good desires, sap our energy, and tap us down, becoming an albatross around our neck. I'm asking you to watch the best YouTube videos, listen to the best audios, and read books like this for the rest of your life. We each need to be lifelong learners and top earners!

Write down five years in advance how much you want to give yourself, and be generous with yourself. What would have happened if Calvin Hunt had not written his goal down? He wouldn't have had the superlative big sale and superstar commission.

Finance has two parts. Most members in America are members of Spenders Anonymous and save what's left. If you are a member of Spenders Anonymous, you're ultimately in a lose-lose situation.

I wrote a little book called *The Miracle of Tithing*, because I'd ask you to start tithing if you have never done so. If need be, start with giving 1 percent of your net income and build up to 10 percent. God's willing to give you 100 percent, but he says if you're operating out of integrity, give 10 percent back to the church, temple, synagogue, ashram, or mosque—the person, place, or thing that sources you spiritually and feeds your soul.

Does that really work? Let me give you my own experience of that. We refinanced one of our income producing rental properties and took out $80,000 cash. My wife and I said, "Is this income or not?" We decided it was income. We immediately wrote a check for eight grand. I don't care how rich you are: writing a check for eight grand makes you have second thoughts. We wrote the check for eight grand and immediately sent it off.

Within three minutes, the banker called back and said, "Remember that $80,000 loan? You, my dear friend, get 2 percent off in interest." Two percent of $100,000 is $2,000 a year, which, times 30 years, is $60,000 for sending in $8,000; we had just tithed. The only explanation of this is supernatural. God is supernatural and knows and sees all.

Scriptural wisdom says: if your giving is in secret, "your Father, who sees in secret, will reward you openly" (Matthew 6:4). What a miraculous truth! You have to experience it to believe it, and it works every time. When I am asked why I sell more books than anyone else alive, I always answer the same way: because I tithe on every book I write and sell. God sees what I am doing and rewards me openly.

Out of 100 percent, you are requested voluntarily to tithe only 10 percent of your net earnings to God. If you've never tried tithing, it opens up your prosperity.

Take the next 10 percent of what you earn, and save it. With your savings, you build up your net worth. Net worth is assets minus liabilities.

At the top of your savings, I put disability insurance. Between ages thirty-five and sixty-five, half of us will be disabled for six months or more. If you've got disability insurance, which really only costs a pittance, they will pay you. When you sign up for it, sign up for a waiver of premium, meaning that you won't have to pay the premium if you become disabled.

Second is life insurance. I recommend that you own a lot. Fifty dollars a month in life insurance is probably worth a million-dollar policy. It doesn't cost much these days to get a million-dollar policy, if you're doing a term policy, which you can convert to whole life as your income grows and expands.

Although I recommend that you start with term insurance, it is a temporary expedient. It's like wetting the bed. It solves the problem temporarily, but over the long term, it has disastrous effects. I'd encourage you to go into universal, variable, or whole life policies if and when you can.

The next idea is to have money in banks. Notice that *banks* is plural. Make sure your bank is profitable. The biggest banks in America are probably the most unstable. If there is a financial crash, which is possible, banks are only FDIC insured for $250,000 per account, so don't have more than that in any one bank account.

I recommend going to a credit union, because they're safe and they're not allowed to lend internationally. They're going to stick around, and they make it easy to get hard loans—as long as you have a history of paying back everything that you have borrowed on. They'll keep lending you more and more.

Art, antiques, and collectibles can be another way of accumulating wealth. Write down all the artists that you want to buy even before you can afford them, and make sure to visit the best art galleries. I had written down that I wanted to buy a Norman Rockwell, because he was the artist who showed Americans at their humorous best. I was in Pennsylvania. I didn't know that's where the Rockwell gallery was. I went in and bought Rockwell's portrait of John F. Kennedy, which I have proudly hanging in my office.

If you want to get rich in art, buy old artists. I have a contract on some of the best artwork produced by the great Western artist Lloyd Austin. For my company, he did the well-known picture of the laughing Jesus, because most people didn't think Jesus smiled or laughed. I don't know if he did, but my experience is that the wisest and smartest people have the best sense of humor.

Decide to get close to artists. We've got many fine artists, who work in many different media. Why don't we recognize them and make them greater by buying their work? Your house, your office, your clinic all deserve to be replete with gorgeous artwork. Artwork is one of the great cultural exchanges we need to do with the whole world.

Stocks, bonds and mutual funds: I knew that the late Lee Iacocca was a winner. At Ford, he did a great job with the Mustang. He comes into Chrysler, takes a derelict, bankrupt, graveyard-destined company, and gives it a purpose statement: "Chrysler will be the biggest and the best."

Under Lee Iacocca's expert and seasoned leadership, Chrysler skyrocketed up. I bought the stock when it was at three. The principle here is buy low, sell high. Know the management of the company, and when you get in, write down when you're getting out. I wrote down I would get out at fifty. Someone might say, "You could have made a lot more money if you held." No: pigs are greedy. They lose every time. There's only one goal in the stock market: make a profit.

By the way, if you know the market's going to go down—and if your inner knower is all-wise and tells you to do so—then buy and sell short. Going long means that your money appreciates; going short means you expect your investment to be worth financially less at a certain point in the future.

There is stock market volatility daily, meaning the market could go up or down. I happen to think the market will keep going up; I don't care what the doomsayers say, although we've got lots of them out there.

Here's why the doomsayers appeal and why their books sell so well: you've only got two motivations in your head.

One is fear, and one is faith. It's easier to hit somebody's hot buttons with fear than with faith and love and joy. But it says in Hebrews 11:1. "Faith is the assurance of things hoped for, the conviction of things not seen."

Gold, silver and diamonds: my recommendation is that you wear them, because if you feel prosperous, you become more prosperous.

Invest in your own business. Warren Buffett, the world's most famous and successful investor, says that the best investment you can ever make is in yourself. Invest in books, classes, seminars, and teachers, so that you know what will happen to what he calls "Mr. Market." The best investment you make is in your own headspace and mindset, because if they're working right, you're working right.

Invest in real estate. The first goal is, invest in your own home. Your goal in real estate investments is to buy your own home, then invest in one single-family property a year. Don't use your money if you can use somebody else's. Buy one house a year for ten years, and you'll be financially free and independent. In the tenth year, refinance the house you bought in the first year, and live on the refinanced money, which is tax-free. The goal of every wealth building person is to live a tax-free lifestyle and to live on the income of one's income.

Why not decide to have a luxurious life and home? It doesn't cost anything to decide that you're going to have a luxurious, glorious, gorgeous home that has everything you want, and then some. If you can't find it, you get to design it. There's plenty of room wherever you want to live.

I'm all for your having multiple homes while you're young and can enjoy them. Taxwise, you can have a first, second, third home: whatever the richest two are, you can write those off. Why? It's not just for billionaires; you can too.

Let's talk about thinking big. I was in Vietnam the same time as Fred Smith, founder of Federal Express. Fred went to Yale University. He wrote a little paper that said that to make packages get delivered absolutely, positively overnight, you have to have a hub system. His business professor said, "That is an asinine idea, Fred Smith, and I am giving you a C minus."

Fred comes back from Vietnam and gets an investment group to put $20 million into building his little company. In two years, Fred proceeds to blow out every dollar because he couldn't put the system together quickly enough. FedEx was his magnificent obsession, his big idea. Fred later told the professor, "You keep the C minus, and I will keep my billions, thank you."

When you go down to his hub in Tennessee, where everything synchronizes, go between 11:00 p.m. and 2:00 a.m. Planes will arrive on any given night with ten million packages daily—a billion to a billion and a half packages a day at Christmas. In three hours, all these trucks go from plane to plane; everything is color-coded in, and out in a flash; it is something to behold. The system makes it possible to do what was previously impossible: deliver packages overnight all the way around the world.

Something that couldn't be done, Fred did. What Fred Smith has had to do was to say, there's always a new way.

Better than that, there's always a way. No matter what the problem is, there's always a solution if you're solution-oriented.

Fred has created the greatest inventory networking system for IBM and other major corporations. Because of Fred's innovative business, all other businesses have been morphed, modified, and vastly improved.

If you go down to Texas, go through the headquarters of Mary Kay Cosmetics. Everything is done by a robot. Somebody types in an order, and a robot picks it, packs it, shifts it, and addresses it. Mary Kay and Fred now can send out a query on everything they want, and it can tell where it is anywhere in the world.

The trick here is, think big. Think big to achieve big.

Money is created in four ways. Number one: *I work*. Work has dignity. It builds self-esteem. Work has class. Work creates self-worth. It creates self-esteem. Please plan on working, and decide to get more out of yourself on a regular basis. I talk about how to outperform yourself, outlead, outserve, outmanage, outwork, outserve, outfinance yourself.

Number two is, *others work*. Get others to work; in other words, delegate rather than stagnate. Hire somebody else to do something that you could do, while you do the things that only you can do, that nobody else can do. Pay somebody else to do all the things that need to be done but for which the labor doesn't cost much. It creates a vacuum behind you, creating new opportunities for employees.

Number three, *money works*. Above I covered the steps of basic investment in a comprehensive, structural way.

Last but not least, *ideas work*. This is where the big money is made with ideas. Years ago, a client of mine called me up and said, "Mark, I've just become marketing director of Sprint." (Since then, in 2020, Sprint merged with T-Mobile.) I said, "Oh, that's great. Congratulations. I'm really proud of you. I'm thankful that they had the vision to see that you're the right person in the right place."

Do you know what *Sprint* stands for? It's an acronym for *Southern Pacific Railway Integrated Network Transmission*. It started with a railroad. The Southern Pacific Railroad operated thousands of miles of track, but it also had thousands of miles of telegraph wire that ran along those tracks. In the early 1970s, the company began looking for ways to use its existing communications lines for long-distance calling. That was part of the beginning of what we know as Sprint.

Decades ago, railroads could have said, "We're not in the railroad business, but in the transportation business." Most railroads said, "No, our mission statement is, we're in the railroad, business," but the Southern Pacific took a different tack.

I'm saying to you, make sure that your prosperity purpose statement is big and inclusive and that you can grow to be all you can become with your written purpose statement.

Sprint delivers most of the poisonous gas in America. It is shipped by rail, because that's the safest way to ship it. For security, they had to develop digital fiber optics. If, God forbid, one of those trains ever tips over, the company knows in a nanosecond and can contain it so it doesn't wipe out a whole city.

Idea equity is one of the greatest things. If you read about the great money accumulators of our time, all of them basically did it with ideas. Each great wealth builder essentially created a Master Mind alliance around them, which helped execute the big idea.

Whatever you want, you can have if you really want it with your all—head and heart. I really would like to do fun things in my head and heart, because if you do, everybody will be attracted to you by your nature, by your effervescence, by your excitement, by your enthusiasm. *Enthusiasm* means the spirit of God within, which is shown without.

Therefore, as I keep repeating, prosperity is an inside job. Prosperity thinking gives you the kind of compensation that leads to unlimited riches and self-replenishing prosperity.

You may say, "You don't understand, Mark, I'm on a fixed income." There's no such thing as fixed incomes, just fixed mindsets. Only you can control your mind. If you truly change your mind to think, feel, and believe, you will become prosperous. The law of attraction kicks in, and voilà! You're prosperous!

God has multiple ways of making you prosperous, but as it says in Romans 11:3, his ways are past finding out. You have to start with a prosperous mindset to create a prosperous money set.

Who's got to take care of your finances? You do. Don't expect Social Security to cover your expenses in retirement. You may say, "I'm married. My spouse earns a lot of money." Yes, that's really nice. Suck it in and tough it out, because your spouse can be fired, die, or become disabled.

Napoleon Hill says if you overdeliver now, you will be overpaid later. Dr. Hill's most famous statement, which I want you to memorize, repeat endlessly, and take ownership of is, "Anything the mind can conceive and believe, you can achieve."

Here's the question to ask yourself. How big is my concept? How big is my life agenda? How rich do I want to become? (It has to be a number, and the number you pick can either have your financial situation ascend or descend, so be wise in your choice.) How meaningful a life do I want to live and fully express my highest and best self?

How wondrous is your belief system, because your belief system is what tests you? Right now there are many great entrepreneurs doing powerful good, like Elon Musk. They've got good walks and talks, but when you get really close to them, you say, "That guy or gal is no smarter than I am." If that person can do it, you can.

Incidentally, that's not meant to be a put-down; it's meant to inspire your aspirations. It's meant to show that most people can do more than they're doing—ten times, a hundred times, or—a thousand times more than they have done.

One of the most entrepreneurial millionaire stories in America is that of little Hub Cap Annie. Annie Utley never made it through the sixth grade. She started collecting hubcaps off the road in Las Vegas. Today, Hub Cap Annie is a major retail franchise for car parts.

It doesn't matter where you start; it matters where you are going and how you are investing your mind, heart, and energy to create your prosperity. Emerson said, "Do the thing, and you'll have the power." I will morph that to say, do the right thinking and you will generate the right results, right here and right now.

Look at Hub Cap Annie's story, and say, "If she can do it, I can do it." She did her thing, and you can do yours. You are coded from birth with a destiny to fulfill and be thrilled.

Another man started Starving Students. I interviewed him. He couldn't go through college, because he had no money to pay his way through and could not secure any financial aid or a scholarship. His parents were have-nots, so it wasn't part of any program they could afford. In 1973, he said to himself, "I'll start a company. I'll call it Starving Students Moving Company." They've had millions of successful moves since then.

There's a franchise called Mr Waffles, where if you come in and work, they'll let you open up the next store and be the manager. Then, after two years of indentured service, you get half of all the profits of the store. There are many deals like that. Once you know they exist and look for them, you will be astounded at how many there are. They'll make you rich if you follow the protocols and think prosperous thoughts.

There are programs involving employee stock options (ESOs), whereby you can get rich with stock. There are many ways for corporations to use life insurance underwriting to guarantee retirement for every employee. If you're thirty years old, save $20 a week, put it in an IRA (investment retirement account), you'll end up with a million and a half dollars at retirement, if you're at a reasonable rate of interest. There are many places now where you can get high interest rates, if you're willing to take a little risk and pay a lot of attention.

All of us are paid in two ways. Most of us think in terms of direct wages. I'm going to suggest that nobody is really on a wage: everybody is on a commission. You may say, "Wait a second, I'm a secretary. I earn $8, $12, or $20 an hour." But if you stop working, you stop getting paid. That's a commission; it's just called a salary to convince you not to be afraid and not to pay what you are truly worth.

The second way that we get paid is experience gained from this occupation. If you really master a moneymaking skill, you can start your own enterprise and get paid all that you are worth. You can do it. The world needs you to do it.

Remember also, whatever you need, everybody else needs. As Norman Vincent Peale said, "Find a need or want and fill it."

Opportunity is everywhere and, as I've already stressed, it is expanding fast as four billion buyers are fast coming online, thanks to cell phones, forty thousand satellites, robots, 3D printing of everything (including body parts), and AI (artificial intelligence.)

All markets are world markets. That means there are eight billion consumers. All you need to do is sell and earn $1 from a product you sell to one billion people and voilà—you are a billionaire.

I really want you to think deductively. As Bucky said, "Think from universe back to world, back to the United States, back to wherever you live. Make sure you think of serving all humanity, because they need it."

Earl Nightingale said that compensation comes out of four factors: How much need is there for what you do? What is your ability to do it? How difficult would it be to replace you? Do people demand only you? That's what you want to do: make yourself indispensable.

11

The World's Largest Paper Clip

How long will we work with a child until they learn to walk? As long as it takes. In the American school system, we are teaching an obsolete industrial model of learning, with a bell curve. Some win, some lose, and the vast majority are in the middle. But everybody can get an A, as I learned from a teacher who was once featured on *Sixty Minutes*.

She started with a class in the ghetto, and by the end of sixth grade, they were doing sophomore and college work, because she reinforced the students positively. She believingly told them they were going to get an A, and they were all going to work hard to help one another all get A's. Everybody helped everybody. If you missed ten questions on a Monday quiz, you could retake it on Tuesday, and again on Wednesday, until you could answer all ten questions right.

I've already mentioned the "Acres of Diamonds" speech that Dr. Conwell gave six thousand times. A farmer paid $10 each for him and his wife to attend. After listening to Conwell, the husband challenged the wife, saying, "You got Conwell's message: one hour of him saying, 'Everybody can be rich,' and you really believe that nonsense. Now, if you're so dang smart, go make us rich." Ooh, did he irritate his wife!

If you look at all the papers from President Abe Lincoln at the Abraham Lincoln Museum and Library, you'll see that there's blood on all of them, because people used to have to pin presidential papers together, and they would stick themselves. This lady saw that. This lady said, "There's a better way to keep these together." She invented the paper clip. If you go to downtown Philadelphia today, you'll see a paper clip monument dedicated to that little lady's imagination. Said to be the biggest paper clip in the world, it goes seven stories into the air.

Just look around. Opportunity is everywhere. It just takes one idea to become prosperous. Most people, when they see an acorn, see an acorn. Some of you see an oak tree. If you're into real estate, you'll see a lot of houses. A zoologist will see a lot of squirrels.

People often confuse efficiency for effectiveness. I'm asking you to go for being effective. That means get the result, because you only get paid for getting results, not for effort.

Again, you must have your priorities in writing.

Write down 101 goals. The good news, is 85 to 90 percent of what you write down will come true easily, effortlessly, and automatically, during the next year in ways you can't even believe, so make sure your goal setting is exciting, dynamic, and purposeful for you. Go for innovation.

One time I was speaking in New York, and I saw a lady on crutches. I don't know what drove me to do it, but I let my subconscious guide me and said, "I see you walking."

Six months later, I went back to talk again to the same audience. The woman came up to me, hugged me, and said, "Do you remember me?"

Actually I didn't, but I smiled and said, "Yes."

"You're the one who said, 'I see you walking,' because you believed I could walk when the doctors didn't. I'm now walking."

It's amazing. You and I can have a tremendous effect on other people. It could be something so simple as a wink or a smile, so make sure you do your pretense for competence, cosmetics for character. These are the things not to sell out on.

We're in an enormously exciting time. We're going to do things perfectly again. There was a great coach named Ron O'Brien in Mission Viejo, California, who trained Olympic diver Greg Louganis.

O'Brien was a pro. He videotaped the kids he coached all the time, but he only showed them the videotapes of when they did their dives perfectly.

People say, "You're a clumsy oaf," or, "You're a dope." They say, "Don't throw the ball low and inside." The subconscious mind can't hear "Don't," so the trainee throws it low and inside.

O'Brien said, "Greg, you've done this dive perfectly 180,000 times, and all you've got to do is do it one more time perfectly. Greg, you're going to do it, aren't you?"

The kid made it. He was watching himself perform flawlessly, so he could perform flawlessly.

Great coaches and great and inspiring teachers can take losers and turn them into winners, because they see that they are winners. The movies to watch about this include *To Sir with Love* and *Stand and Deliver.*

Everybody's a winner if they've got a great coach or teacher. If you don't, get them in the form of books, videos, audios, and seminars. Hang out with them and become Master Mind partners with them. Assure your employees a decent standard of living. Each of us has to cost-effectively innovate.

Right now, touch yourself and say, *I'm state of the art and state of the future.*

When you're doing your prosperity building, why not be state of the art? And better yet, state of the future? Why not decide to do it more exquisitely and excitingly than you've ever done it before? As I've already empha-sized, the gift of giving is receiving. I reap and experience what I sow in consciousness generously, creatively, boldly, with an attitude of gratitude, and it will return gener-ously.

You've got to see, feel, believe, and take action. "Do the thing and you have the power," Emerson said, "toward your evolving prosperity."

To increase my prosperity consciousness, I must increase somebody else's. I teach what I most need to learn, and it returns to me in every direction, or omni-directionally. If you need more prosperity, start teaching prosperity. If you learn one point out of today, teach it to somebody else whom you think would benefit from hear-ing and learning that one point. Best of all, it will lock into you the edification that you truly desire.

Another moneymaking idea is to become an intrapre-neur: an individual with entrepreneurial spirit who sells a stellar idea to a big, branded company that can profitably distribute and market the product or service. Dr. Arthur Fry at 3M Company invented Post-it notes, and they sell fifty billion a year. As an intrapreneur he contracted to earn 1 percent for any profit made by Post-it Notes.

If you say, "I can't do a company myself," you don't have to. Master Mind, and become an intrapreneur, because companies either live or die based on their innovations. Come up with a great idea or innovation that works, take it to a big and important, brand-name distributor, go with a superstar agent, and get an everlasting contract that pays into perpetuity.

My enjoyment of prosperity increases my prosperity. What does that mean? If you've only got $1 to spend, circulate it with joy and happiness. Take that store chain Pick 'n Save. The poorest person, with only a few bucks in his or her pocket, can go into Pick 'n Save and feel rich. You can go into Pick 'n Save and come out with treasures for nothing.

How would you like to get a new wardrobe very inexpensively? I learned this originally from my wife and from inspirational author Dr. Catherine Ponder. It says if you want a new wardrobe, go through your wardrobe at least quarterly. Take your Post-its and put them on all your clothes, marking them on a scale of 1 to 10, with the exception of the stuff that has sentimental value, like the dress you got married in. If anything has less than an 8, get rid of it by giving it to Salvation Army, Goodwill, or a charitable and honorable thrift store that truly helps those in need.

Give your possessions with joy. If you don't give out your retired clothes, jewelry, glasses, shoes, and household items, with a joyful heart and soul, new clothes, shoes, and other artifacts can't come back with joy. What goes out comes back, many times in spontaneous, surprising, and sudden ways.

Give away your old clothes. Amazing things happen. My wife and I, when we first got married, went to a late-night movie. Back then, we didn't have cabs running twenty-four hours a day in our vicinity. When we got out, I saw the lights of my car were very dim. My wife said, "You don't think I'm going to walk home, do you?"

"Oh, and how *are* you getting home?"

Next morning, I come back out to jump-start the car, and in front of me, I see a store that says, "All fine clothes, 10 percent or less of original retail." They had Brioni, Givenchy, Canali, Ferragamo, and all the best men's clothes and shoes.

I went in and bought a fantastic wardrobe, all because I'd created a vacuum. If you create a vacuum, something's got to fill it, so if you get rid of the old clothes, new clothes will magically arrive and takes their place. There may be a little or no price tag on them. Somebody will give them to you as a gift. There's a million ways they can show up. They can show up in all kinds of ways.

In Southern California, there's an event called First Thursday. All the great stars up in LA, like Cher, give their clothes to First Thursday, and luxury clothing manufacturers give their overruns. They sell them incredibly inexpensively, and all the money goes to charity.

One year I had written down as one of my 101 goals to get a tuxedo. Although I can afford one, but I didn't want to go out and circulate that much money, my need was not high, and I wasn't in a rush. I just wrote down, "I want a tuxedo" one day.

When I came back home, my wife had been to First Thursday and said, "I just got you a $925 tuxedo for $25." All the tailor had to do is finish my cuffs, and I was home free and dressed to the nines.

It's just that quick. Why? Because if you keep giving, amazing clothes keep showing up.

Another prosperity point is that you've got to have good time control. To have good time control, to save time and quickly launch your day, I recommend that you organize your clothes the night before, so you can just take your shower and dress. While you're taking your shower, I hope you fluff your aura and sing to yourself positively, "I'm prosperous, I'm happy, I'm one with God," and then move with alacrity and finesse into your day.

How do you get energy? You decide to be energetic. This has a lot of aspects to it. I used to drive Bucky Fuller home to the dome he lived in while he taught at Southern Illinois University. I'd be driving him home at 2:30 a.m. I'd be bleary-eyed, and Bucky would say, "Be back to pick me up at 4:30 a.m." At the time, I was twenty-one, and he was seventy-one, and I'd mentally go, "You're kidding." I'd be back, and he'd always be ready, but I didn't understand how he did it. I finally said, "Do you meditate?" He says, "Mark, don't you understand? I live in meditation. I'm in my right livelihood. This is what I'm supposed to do.

"What I want you to understand, my boy, is that you don't own you. Universe owns you and you're here to serve Universe. You get to be an extension of me, and you're temporarily serving me until you learn it so you can do it."

"What do you do when you go to sleep at night?" I asked. "Give me some of the simple, pragmatic stuff of how you have all this energy, so you only sleep two hours a night."

"First of all, you only need one ninety-minute shot of deep sleep at night. When you go into sleep, you never say you're tired until three seconds before you nod off. See, most people wake up in morning, and they say, 'Oh, my God. I didn't sleep last night. I'm so tired.' They are mentally malpracticing, and then they wonder why they get the wrong result. Before you go to sleep, tell yourself, 'I'm going into deep sleep instantly.' Then tell yourself, 'I'm going to wake up totally, absolutely refreshed.'"

W. Clement Stone taught me two things about how to end procrastination. First of all, he said to end procrastination, take your hands out, smash them together, and make them sting. Then say, *Do it now*. Do this twelve times in a row. Then you take the action.

He also advised, "Every morning when I wake up, say to yourself, 'I feel healthy, I feel happy, I feel terrific.'"

Once you say you're energized, you're going to start eating better foods. You're going to start taking in the vitamins that are appropriate for you.

As a success philosopher, I say you've got to have too many goals. Napoleon Hill taught that you've got to have one definite major purpose. What we didn't understand at that time is that multiphasic intelligence works in non-simultaneous, only partially overlapping parts. Different goals will have different realization time frames, just like living things: a chicken egg has a gestation period of twenty-one days; a human embryo, nine months; an elephant, two years.

Once you have 101 goals written down, on the left-hand side, prioritize them emotionally, on a scale of 1 to 10. You put your white-hot desire, your magnificent obsession, onto a higher level of prioritization. Shut your eyes and say, which of these things is most important to me now, and which ones can I realize? Unless your mind is suffering from self-sabotaging erroneous zones, it'll go snap! and that's what you're hot about. Write your goals in the *I am this* and *I have this* forms.

Let me tell one little story. Back in fifteenth-century Germany, there was a father that had fifteen children. He loved the children so much that he worked three jobs just to make sure that all of them got fed.

The last two were boys. They talked, and they both said they wanted to go to the great Nuremberg art academy and become artists. There's no way their dad, working around the clock, could ever have created enough prosperity for them to do it.

The boys agreed that one of them would go into the coal mines and work as many shifts as it took. The other would go to the Nuremberg academy, using the money earned from the coal mine, and create great renown as an artist.

The brother that went into the art academy was quickly a sensation. Every piece of work he did was a masterpiece. All the teachers did was teach him finesse and refinement.

As this brother was ready to graduate, his father pulled out all the stops and invited all his family members and neighbors to a great hoedown. He said, "I want to congratulate you, my dear sons, who have empowered our whole family. I totally love both my sons, Albrecht and Albert Dürer."

The great artist was Albrecht. The father said, "Albrecht, I'm so enamored of what you've done. I want to toast you in front of everybody that's here."

Albrecht says, "Sweet father of mine, I appreciate you toasting me for my artwork, but I could not have done it unless my loving brother Albert had not gone into the mines. What we need to do here is to praise him. I've made enough money with one commission that I can afford to send him to the academy."

Albert stood up with tears pouring out of his eyes and said, "Sweet brother of mine, I've been in the mines working two shifts a day, seven days a week, so you could go to school. During that time, I contracted such gnarling arthritis that I cannot open my hands, much less go to art school."

Albrecht responded, "It is out of my complete love for you that I painted these praying hands pointing towards the sky, to permanently show the enormity of your complete sacrifice, so I could become an artist. You will never be forgotten."

Albrecht's masterpiece *Praying Hands* is known around the world. In deference to his brother, he drew the praying hands, of which you yourself may have a copy.

I'm suggesting to you that prosperity is an inside job, but you don't get to do it alone. We only get to do it if we participate, integrate, and do it with other people. Albert's love and devotion to Albrecht gave us *Praying Hands*. You can see that love was a force of dedicated love, respect, appreciation.

I am dedicated to seeing more in you today than perhaps you see in yourself. Remember, I am always cheering you on to higher heights of success, love, joy, riches, and fulfillment of your destiny. Instead of each of us being alone, we are here to be all one. The spirit in me honors the spirit in you.

12

How to Adapt

Charles Darwin, who famously taught the principle of survival of the fittest, said, "It is not the strongest of the species that survives, nor the most intelligent. It is the one that is most adaptable to change."

We all know that in hurricanes, trees either bend and survive or break from their rigidity. During any challenge, we must be bendable, pivotable, and transformational to survive. These tips will serve to make sure that you can bend a bit under the pressures that come, but never break.

Today we are called upon to think, move, adapt, and transform better, faster and with more wisdom than at any time in human history. It's only the most adaptable to change who survive. If you are wise and ready to adapt and change, you will go far beyond survival to fully thriving.

In this book, I'm sharing important information for you, whether you're in a pandemic, recession, or personal crisis, or are just starting over. Life throughout the ages has always been fraught with challenges and opportunities. Throughout history, life has presented humankind with trials and tribulations of every sort, including floods, earthquakes, fires, epidemics, blights, plagues, and market crashes. Our ancestors always survived and ultimately thrived.

We will do the same. To do so, we need to have the most practical insights, wisdom, and information available. This book is intended to serve as a handy reference guide through such times. The simple truths contained within can be your guiding compass to staying well, safe, and on track, and most importantly, coming away stronger, better, and more prepared for life.

I also want to inspire you with foundational hope that can support your transformational journey. Hope incentivizes us to stay alive, go through the struggles and adversities, and arrive advantaged in the end.

Keep this book handy, and share it with all that you love. I offer it to you in hopes that you can not only survive but thrive in bigger and better ways than ever.

I am going to give you the big picture that I envision will happen as we exit the pandemic crisis. I am predicting there will be grand opportunities and some challenges to go with them. Today, and through every challenge, big thinking is essential, because our thinking must be bigger than our problems.

Let me discuss two major symbols that you are probably familiar with since childhood. One is the ancient symbol of the yin and the yang. It has survived in our memory for over six thousand years, because the principle behind it is verifiably true.

In lay language, this symbol is to be interpreted as CRISIS = OPPORTUNITY. As I write this, we are in the biggest crisis ever—the Covid pandemic—and therefore we can also see it is the biggest opportunity ever, if we are awake, thoughtful, and positive, and choose to transform.

The other is the butterfly, because butterflies are the universal symbol of freedom. My companies and books, like *The One Minute Millionaire*, have always had the symbol of the butterfly emblazoned on them. As you adapt wisely, you are now in a position to increase your freedom. Remember, you cannot look at a caterpillar and predict a butterfly. Nor can you look at the crisis that had eight billion people simultaneously in lockdown without seeing that a butterfly is about to emerge from a total cocoon.

Since 1776 and the Articles of Confederation, we have had forty-seven recessions and two major depressions: in 1893–98, and in 1929–39. After the depression in the 1890s, four innovations created the new industrial America: the automobile, electricity, the telephone, and the airplane. After the Great Depression of the 1930s came

TV, jet planes, and ultimately the computer. The computer started seriously evolving with Dr. Gordon Moore's law, which says that processor speeds, or overall processing power for computers, will double every two years and basically halve in price. That fact made computers, smartphones, and the Internet possible.

After every contraction—whether it be a recession or depression—there is vast and virtually immediate, profitable, and almost invisible expansion from technological breakthroughs.

We will make it through this crisis, and as we have done with every crisis or setback, we will be better off when it is over. We have extraordinary opportunities looming for those that are awake and willing to proceed with vigor. Yes: you will have to reset your thinking, pivot, create plan B, and decide to contribute in new ways.

Companies that were unknown and unheard of a decade ago are now worth billions, such as Uber, Airbnb, Instagram, and Square. I predict that hundreds more are being conceived as you read this. Signings of documents have gone completely electric with DocuSign, which is worth over $100 billion. Important papers are now instantaneously signed and deals are finalized with buyers and sellers never even seeing each other or entering what five years ago was called a closing room.

These all came from ideas born from individuals trying to solve problems or make something better. Perhaps you are the creative innovator who will positively transform our world.

The question you have to ask yourself again is, how am I going to participate in this colossal change? What can I personally do that I will love doing and be paid substantially for so doing? Or what needs fixing, and am I capable of creating or being on a team that does it?

Here is some of what is happening, before our very eyes, that will vastly shape the future:

The world is now videocentric and podcasting-centric, with people running over ten million meetings per day through Zoom from their homes or offices. 5G is increasingly available, and we'll soon have pop-up 3D avatars of people emerging in holographs out of your phone in real time. The seven biggest innovations that I believe and predict will do $50 trillion worth of business from 2020 to 2030 in America include but are not limited to:

Turning Trash to Cash with QCI LLC in Michigan. QCI can recapture almost 99 percent every atom and molecule from our garbage and landfills, thus creating millions of jobs, unlocking trillions of dollars in needed but frozen resources, ending most pollution, ending the poisoning of our water supplies, giving us back virtually unlimited fuel, metal, plastic, pure water, and saving the earth from contamination and waste.

We are advisors to QCI and see the technology playing a huge role in the management of waste, turning it into an important monetizable resource in the near future.

AI is artificial intelligence or supercomputation. We see it in our smartphones' GPS systems and when you "ask Google" or the equivalent systems. You punch it in, and it is your talking road map. It will be making millions of transactions in a nanosecond Like Thomas Watson, the late president of IBM, we can see that the human mind can't think that fast. However, humans are needed to really think, be ethical, make decisions, and choose from the options AI will quickly give us.

5G will be superfast and will take downloadability to virtual instantaneity. You will, for example, be able to download complete three-hour movies into your computer or smartphone while traveling on a jet forty thousand feet in the air. Each telephone company tells us that they are the fastest and best. It is a big race, and we will soon all know the winner.

Natural Power Concepts in Oahu, Hawaii, started by being an alternative energy device invention and design company (www.natural powerconcepts.com). John Pitre, the artist, inventor, and genius behind it, has 250 world-improving inventions to create urban wind with stream auger turbines and pulsing wave technology. He is working to create integrated energy storage—in his Wind Charger innovation. This is green technology at its best. I am a founder, investor, and co-owner.

Robots and cobots. Robots will do all the menial, hard, disgusting, and impossible work formerly relegated to blue-collar workers. Soon we will have cobots (collaborative robots) doing the work no one wanted to do and elevating menial labor into running bots and becoming vastly more productive, better trained, and higher paid.

This trend will not destroy but create jobs. Steve Forbes suggests that it will create twenty-two million new jobs in this decade. As Warren Buffett says: a hundred years ago, 98 percent of Americans were farmers, and 2 percent were white-collar. The fear was that if work transitioned out of agriculture, everyone would be out of work. Today, 98 percent of Americans are not farmers, 2 percent are farmers, and the economy is better than ever. With bots, the economy will be even more productive and profitable, and everyone will be happier.

The IoT (the Internet of things) will connect fifty billion devices. Your phone, computer, home, car, and other apparatus will be connected virtually. It's hard to believe, but only fifteen years ago, no one thought we could all disconnect from telephone landlines, but all of us have done that and more.

Multidimensional transportation: we are all moving from 2D to 3D travel. Flying cars are no longer science fiction. I have seen them and sat in them at the Consumer Electronic Show. I have sat with their inventor from Boeing, Charlie Spinelli. They will be safer than what we travel in now. It will probably have a name like Uber Air. This trend will end traffic congestion, speed travel, and be run on electric batteries, thus eliminating a lot of pollution.

As a result of the pandemic, we have realized that we must take more control of our supply chains and manufacturing, rather than outsourcing important products and services we rely on for our health, safety, and well-being. In the coming years there will be tremendous opportunities in manufacturing, distribution, and all aspects of the supply chain. The twenty-year contraction in these areas will now be met with a gigantic resurgence, making jobs and opportunities plentiful for all, if we're awake, informed, and enthused.

Will all of this happen? Only time will tell. I think most of it will, and a whole lot more. Will we have obstacles to surmount? Of course, yes! We will go over, under, around, and through every conceivable obstacle. However, Americans have brilliant, innovative ingenuity, determination to action, and grit. We will stay and continue to be the brave beacon on a hill, offering bravery and opportunity. Our overall habits of happiness, an invincible work ethic, and positively creative marketing will prevail.

A great deal of naysaying media is available for our consumption, because show producers think that drama and bad news sells. The truth is, there is infinitely more good news than bad news. Also, be advised to limit your intake of negative news to 15 minutes a day. More news than that hurts your psyche, thinking, and your future.

Look what happened in recent years, when our political leadership came together and voted for a $2 trillion bailout to help Americans get through these tough times. The only way to succeed is through cooperation and innovation. New ideas in the spirit of cooperative harmony will get us through this trial and help us rebound triumphantly.

Remember, the last four letters of the word American are I CAN. We can and we will prevail and thrive.

13

A Meditation

On audio, I lead a creative visualization experience. Here you can enjoy reading, absorbing, and contemplating it. You can read it aloud, record it, and play it back to yourself, or turn on music and have another read it to you. You should not listen to it while you're driving a car or handling heavy machinery.

For best results, be in a relaxed position in your bed, on the floor or on your favorite chair. Create a space of relaxed, uninterrupted awakeness. If you can, add music by Steven Halpern or crystal bowl music or meditation music. Here are the words of one meditation on unlimited riches. Now close your eyes and repeatedly internalize these ideas and thoughts to yourself.

I close my outer eyes, and I open my inner eyes. I breathe in a good breath of life. I feel good all over. I feel magnificent. I am happy about myself at the fiber of my being. I am experiencing and expressing unlimited riches. Riches are me. I open a screen of my imagination, and I see myself the way I want to be. I tilt my inner eye up at a twenty-degree angle. I am at a new perfect level of beingness.

My awareness and creativity are heightened to the maximum. My inner being is awakening to new financial realizations. I have a positive, productive, creative, money-getting psychology. My mind is aware of abundant opportunities. My mind is self-organizing in exciting new ways. I feel unlimited riches coming to and through me, right here and right now. New positive, profitable ideas are flowing into me. I know they work, and my mind grasps them. I capture them on paper. I look at them. I tingle all over. This is good stuff. I review them regularly. I feel good about them. I maintain my eager enthusiasm to realize them.

I attract into my experience the people I need to fulfill my dreams, desires and good ambitions. My life overflows with health, wealth, riches, joy, and happiness. I am contributing at my highest and best. I am forever conceiving new ways to contribute. I'm inventing new markets and new market processes. I'm creating new marketplaces. It feels good. My great new ideas are employing ever more people. I can see it. It's working. I'm outpicturing what I've been inpicturing.

My big ideas are exciting and awakening the rest of humanity. I feel it, I believe it, I expect it, and I fulfill it. I feel deeper wisdom with new, inspired creativity exploding within me and without. I make a profound difference. I feel and see my highest vision for myself is now being realized. My highest vision for humanity is now being realized.

I turn the noes I've heard into yeses. The universe only says yes to me. I hear echoing in my mind's eye and ear, "Yes, yes, yes, yes, yes." I turn all disadvantages into advantages. I am rejection-proof. I'm earning great wealth by wisely leveraging my investments of time, money, and effort. I am earning millions, and I see my millions earning millions.

I know and use all the principles of success. *I can* and *I will* are my only credos. I go first-class, with style, dignity, grace, courage, excellence, and elegance. I feel elegant inside and outside. Going first-class is its own best revenge. I go first-class. I am visiting all the great places with all the great people. I am with locals that give me the inside tour.

My dreams are being fulfilled now. My dreams are having dreams. They're sparkling. They're beautiful. They dance in my imagination. They're exquisitely being fulfilled. In this golden age, I am making a profound and significant and meaningful difference. I am positively, correctly, and insightfully impacting my life and the life of everyone on the planet. I see new realities—wonderful, blissful, joyous, unfolding new realities. I'm creating them in my mind, and I like it. I gently bite my lip to make sure I'm staying alive as all this good inundates my life.

My life is under constant self-improvement, and I like it. It's getting better and better and better in every wonderful way. My persistence is paying off and paying off and paying off some more. My life is a favorable treat to me and to all others. Others want to bask in energy radiance that I am now easily and effortlessly projecting. I see my every investment appreciating, paying dividends, and it's fun. It's not how much I spend or have spent, but how I spend it and what value I get for it. I am valuable, and that which I do is valuable.

I have confidence in my mind, body, and spirit. I am empowered and empowering. My every word empowers, enriches, and enlivens all those who get close to me. I have the money power to be, do, and have all the good that I desire. My bank accounts are full and drawing interest. Ooh, look at that savings account! I have more in my savings account than I have ever had before. I know there's more coming, and more after that. I am in the divine circulation of my money. Everything that I have, earn, invest, and circulate is multiplied and leveraged and increased and is evolving into more. It feels good at the depth of my being.

My bills are paid off and up, and still I have all that money. Money and riches keep gushing in. I'm current on all accounts. Every month that I see that all my bills are paid in full. I have the best credit. Banks are asking me to borrow their money. It feels so good. It's wonderful. It's a deliciously delightful experience that I want to savor, have, and continue feeling.

I am debt-free. I've paid off the mortgage on my home and my second home. I've paid off my cars, and look at those dazzling, shining, gleaming new automobiles. They are all mine. I feel just a little bit better getting inside, holding the notches on that steering wheel, knowing that I own this car, and it's mine and my family's.

I eagerly raise lots and lots of money for the good causes that I believe in. I am charitable, and I feel good about the charities that I support. No matter where I am or what I'm doing, I'm always looking for and discovering new moneymaking opportunities.

I receive invitations from the who's who of society. I'm on life's A party lists. I'm there because I've chosen to be there. When I give someone one of my picture business cards, it shows what I do with excellence and elegance. I say, "Put me on your A party list." I know which invitations to accept and which to graciously reject. I accept if I choose to.

I occupy a new space of greater respect and more importance for myself, those that are my associates, my society, and my world. I contribute greatly in the spaces that I occupy locally, nationally, and internationally. I love the contributions I make. My mind is zesty with rich, wonderful, unfolding contributions.

I've been down, and now I'm up. Up is definitely better, and up is where I'll stay. I am meeting exciting personalities as an equal. I am meeting the great businesspeople, the great artists, the great musicians, the great scientists, the great and inspiring teachers, who get me into subjects I didn't even know about. I was ignorant, informationally destitute, and they expand my mind, being, and my understanding. I am being fully and completely illuminated.

I'm with media folks in an omnifavorable way. I'm with great world leaders and politicians. I'm with world transformers, world informers, changemakers, transformers, and I am one of them. I am being photographed constantly with the world's who's who. It's a normal, natural experience. The pictures come into my office, I frame them, and I hang them. The energetic resonances of all those people who have decided to be disciplined and on purpose uplift me all who look at them. They give us new feelings of hopefulness and new feelings of helpfulness, and I proudly hang those photos on my wall.

I visualize being with people that I want to be with, enjoy ecstasy and serving for the sake of serving, loving for the sake of loving, opening up my heart energy in new and more profound ways of serving greatly with love. I am dancing to the beat of the universe. My friends and mentors are introducing me to ever-widening circles of people whom I need and want to meet, when I need to meet them, and occasionally before I need to meet them. This exposure and these contacts are giving me access to the area and the arenas of gossip and power that open doors and guarantees my future successes, guarantees future business, future orders for me and those with whom I associate.

I am part of all the great events of this world. I am there right before they happen. I am making the world better for this and all future generations. The radar of my mind is always scanning people, scanning events, scanning circumstances for new openings into the veil and the wall of success. I penetrate to the other side and pull back into full realization that which I choose to have. I have the fire of burning desire inside me, glowing and showing, radiant, magnificently alive. It dances in my solar plexus. It illumines my heart. It is in the healing touch that I put on someone with a word or my hand or even the caress of my eye or the embrace of my energy orbit.

Whether I'm with one, one thousand, one hundred thousand, or a million on TV, my life force energy magnetizes them, uplifts them, energizes them, encourages

them, and excites them to new heights, new levels of fulfillment. As I think this, I see it as a drop in the great pool
of life. The Doppler effect goes out in wave propagation,
infusing all others, going meaningfully, impactfully, and
purposefully into the universe.

It feels good. I'm glad. I'm good to myself. I'm good
to all others. I'm good to the friendly cohabitants of our
little spaceship called earth. I am making a difference
to our world. I'm healing myself. I'm healing our world.
I am part of the unlimited riches that are awakening in
every individual. I know that as I find the riches inside
me, I find the riches of my world outside. It feels good
and very, very good. I'm sharing this insight with everyone. Everyone is coming into the dawning realization
that we're in a new age, a new time, a new level of exquisite excitement where all of us can be and become all
we're meant to be.

Now I live in a spectacular home. It's everything I
ever dreamed I wanted. It's cozy. It's comfortable. It has
exclusive, original artwork adorning my walls. It has
large, expansive windows. It's spacious, it's gracious, it's
palacious. The furniture is what I've always dreamt that
I would comfortably be embraced by and supported by.
I have the TV screen that I wanted, and I coproduce the
media that I want to watch. As a videophile, I only let
enter the portal of my consciousness that which I know
will resonate with my highest level of being. I let them

pervade and fill the interspaces of my mind, uplift me and help me to realize my future.

As I enter the kitchen of my home, it's marvelously spacious. I have a gourmet kitchen. I have sunlight streaming into the floor-to-ceiling windows. I have plants adorning the wall of my kitchen. It feels good. The vibrations here could be that of the most exemplary gourmet cook in the world. It inspires me to create nutritious, healthful breakfasts, lunches, and dinner that have me stay in high, fit healthfulness.

As I go through the rest of my home, I enter into my study. It's book-lined. Tens of thousands of books that I've read and that have become part of me. I become that which I read, and I read the best, which makes me the best. I live in the metaphorical dance of the great minds and the great thinking of all time. It feels good in here. The rug is the color of high spirituality. The wallpaper embraces the clouds, the globe. It puts me into heavenly state.

I have a globe, which I can spin as I think about serving total humanity and selling, serving, mass-producing, and mass-distributing, mass-marketing, and having mass consumption of all that I want to contribute.

Now I walk down the halls, and I see glowing pictures of my family members. They're radiant. Each has its own aura. My heart dances as it remembers capturing the beauty of the moment on film. My eyes well up with tears as I feel love for all my family members.

As I go by my studio, I look at the top of my bookshelf and more pictures of me and those with whom I participate in making a difference.

Now as I walk down the stairs of my abode, I see the pictures of those that I'm romantically involved with. One of the pictures has my beloved sweetheart of a wife, and I feel that joyous, feeling of being one with God and all good.

As I enter the portal called my sacred bedroom, it is spacious. It has an exquisitely expensive quilt of radiant flowers. This is a place where I feel good. The bed is firm. I enter into sleep with a sound system that brings forth subliminal music that lets my mind dance into the fullness of the universe. It peacefully tranquilizes my spirit, mind, and body, rejuvenating me, so I can be a peak performer each and every day.

I've got my windows open, taking in the fresh air from all the herbal and organic plants that surround my environment. I breathe in deeply the sweet smell of the night pine fragrance and the night-blooming jasmine, calming lavender scents, and the lilacs. I smell the wafting lemon tree in season. In my bedroom, I have roses next to my bed, and it gives positive feelings to my vibratory calmness.

When I rise in the morning, caressed by the sweet kiss of the sun, I open the glass door and look out at my estate. I smell the morning bloom of gardenia. It's so nice. I love it. I have a smile on my face, a smile in my heart, and know that my spirit is smiling, happy, and deeply grateful. I feel a great sense of personal satisfaction as I realize my loftiest aspirations and fulfill my highest hopes with a caress of the wisdom of all time, and so it is. It cannot be otherwise. I rejoice because thank you, thank you, thank you.

CPSIA information can be obtained
at www.ICGtesting.com
Printed in the USA
JSHW040452110921
18608JS00001B/1

9 781722 503604